Chosen to be Blessed

Three Secrets to Transform Your Life's Storms to Blessings

Ronald David Re

www.ProphesyLife.com

Printed in the United States of America
Published by Author Academy Elite
P.O. Box 43, Powell, OH 43035
www.AuthorAcademyElite.com

EBook edition created 2016

ISBN: 194352601X
ISBN-13: 9781943526017

Library of Congress Cataloging-in-Publication Data is available upon request.
Edition 2

To protect the privacy some of those who have shared their stories with the author, some details and names have been modified.

Dedication

For Nicole, daddy loves you. Blessed are you
who have not seen and believed in the Lord!

And for all my tribe: God is with you in your storm and sorrow,
run to Him as your strong tower! You are ***Chosen to be Blessed***

"This is a fabulous story of truly amazing grace, dressed up to look like a set of incredible coincidences. This spoke powerfully of the way God is always present in the times of trauma and holds us completely fast, unfazed by our choices and troubles. Ronald lends us the wisdom of his experience generously from the deep reserves of restoration he has forged. You will undoubtedly be encouraged to count your own blessings"

Gill Scott – *Disentangling Genius,* Learning Community Facilitator, Writer and Coach, United Kingdom: www.disentanglinggenius.com

"After we give our lives to Christ we can find that our life is simpler and more fulfilling, but not necessarily easier. Ronald addresses this tension in his book and his personal stories and the lessons can help anyone manage the tension between the promises of God and the pain of the present. Chosen to be blessed is full of wise insights that will encourage any reader who purchases this book!"

Tim Walk – High School Pastor at Mount Paran Church. Atlanta, Georgia. @walkthetim Blog: www.YouthPastorU.org

"How do I face the storms of life and remain on my feet long after they are gone? Ronald not only answers this question but also provides practical steps to becoming **'better instead of bitter'** as a result. This is a must read for all stages of life regardless if there is a present storm in your life or not."

Jeff Stimpson – Teaching & Discipleship Pastor of Grace Church Powell, Ohio

"An Honest, courageous and committed look at turning your challenges into blessing. ...Ronald's story inspires readers to discover new opportunities when braving life's toughest storms."

Robin Nickerson –*THE APEX LIFE*, Speaker, Coach, & Author. Calgary, Alberta: http://www.robinnickerson.com

"Learn practical steps to prepare for life's hardships from Ronald's storms of life. This is a must read in any season of life that will inspire you to follow hard after Jesus no matter what life throws at you."

Jim Spelman –Pastor of Marion Grace Brethren Church, Marion, OH

"In *Chosen to be Blessed*, Ronald Re openly, honestly, and humbly deals with the treacherous events that sometimes blast our lives, our hopes, our dreams. What was thought to be a very happy life with a good future, suddenly erupted into a tortuous series of disheartening and draining experiences. As his secure world was breaking apart, Ronald's analytical mind found its way to probe the wisdom of God, and the transformation it produced in his life is spectacular. With a heart for others whose lives are being shattered with unexplainable hardships, he carefully and clearly lays out the path he took to come to the realization that even disease, death, and divorce, or any other disaster in life, can be turned into unnumbered and ongoing blessings by our redeeming God."

Rev. Ronald Graef – Retired Pastor of Evangel Baptist Church.
Taylor, Michigan

"A gripping portrait of vulnerability and authenticity...Ronald's guidance to transform storms into blessings displays conviction led by his faith in God. *Chosen to be blessed* will guide readers to look at their own adversities and know they are not alone!"

Louise A. Elliott – Leadership & Career Coach, Speaker,
Trainer, and Author. Westerville, Ohio

Contents

Foreward

Ronald David Re's story reads like an amazing tale of fiction, except for one small thing. It's 100% true.

I'm sure in the midst of *living* his story there were times he wished to God it was fiction.

Imagine a young parent receiving earth-shattering news—your little girl has a terminal illness. Although on the outside she appeared vibrant and full of life, on the inside her body was shutting down.

Naturally, this news will bring any couple to their knees.

But what happens if your spouse turns to you in the midst of that storm and informs you of another deathblow—an unexpected divorce will soon be your reality. The one relationship you thought would sustain you through the journey of burying your child is now another loss you must grieve.

Although Ronald's story begins here—devoid of hope and joy, it's not the final chapter. Instead, he takes us deep into a story of reinvention and redemption. Within these pages you'll encounter 3 secrets Ronald discovered in the midst of his storm. These truths helped him emerge full of hope and healing.

Who hasn't wondered why "bad" things happen to "good" people? Chosen to Be Blessed reveals a powerful perspective on this perplexing paradox—How can a good God allow evil?

Join Ronald as he courageously reveals how God is always working on your behalf—beyond what you can imagine—especially in the storms of life.

Kary Oberbrunner

CEO of *Redeem the Day* and *Igniting Souls*. Co-creator of *Author Academy Elite*.

Author of *Day Job to Dream Job, The Deeper Path,* and *Your Secret Name*

Introduction:
Hiding Under the Stars

"Moses answered the people, "Do not be afraid. Stand firm and you will see the deliverance the Lord will bring you today. The Egyptians you see today you will never see again. The Lord will fight for you; you need only to be still."

Exodus 14:13-14

❧ *CHILDISH BELIEF* ❧

We see our relationships with each other that take trust, faith, belief, and hard work to get to know each other. We strive for peace, love, and harmony. Why would we not think a relationship with God takes the same effort? God's goodness is in our humanity by the selfless love of a child, the loyalty of friendship, the sacrifice of a friend and the power of someone that believes in me. We often fail at these and to be perfect is unnatural. However, it points the way for us to search for a bigger reason. Why are we here and what does God have planned for each of us? In Celine Dionne's song **Because you loved me**, she gives the credit to who she is because someone believed in her:

"…You saw the best there was in me…You gave me faith 'coz you believed
I'm everything I am, ***because you loved me."***

If you have someone in your life like this, then you feel truly blessed. When I was young that was my mom. When we hit bottom in the lowest point of the storms of life it is hard to believe that God is still good and on our side. We need someone to believe in us because we have lost strength to believe in ourselves. In the pit of despair, we need friends, family, and others to surround us with love and belief that we will make it through. We also need God to show us a way out of our pain. We are looking for a path of blessings and belief in Him during the storm. **Friends and others can help by believing in us. What makes the bigger difference is when we realize God believed in us first.**

CLEANSING LOVE AND COMFORTING LOVE

When someone has lost blood through a tragic event, he or she needs a blood transfusion. Someone externally adds blood to their system, helping them to heal.

The power of you finding your reason can be seen best when you do a LOVE TRANSFUSION to others.

When you understand and accept God's love you can authentically share what God has done in your life without shame. By being real we can give to others a relatable and comforting love. By understanding the miracles God has done in our life, we can believe a miracle to happen for others. By believing the best in them, like God believed the best in you. This energizes and gives someone a view of their new life, a new perspective and hope that they too can believe better for themselves than what they see - **because you believe in them**.

This has happened to each of us: someone loves you enough to see the best in you even when you were not behaving the best or could only see your failures. For me, that was my mom who believed in me that I could do anything I put my mind to with God's help. This is an example of a positive self-fulfilling prophecy. God did this for all of us that believe in Jesus as savior. He believed in us while we were still sinners: He gave us faith because He believed.

I am everything I am because God loved me.

My RN wife explained different blood treatments that remind me of this concept. She explained the difference between dialysis and a blood transfusion. We can give a love transfusion to comfort and help heal each other, but only Jesus work internally in the heart - can clean the blood, like dialysis... We need both a Cleansing Love and Comforting Love. Our spiritual blood can only be "cleaned" or cleansed from sin by the work of Jesus and His spirit in our lives. When others care for us when we are hurting they give a love transfusion. When we believe in God to save us we experience a cleansing of our blood from sin. Both of these processes save us from life's storms and lead to God's blessings. Many times in life others love transfusions are not enough. We need the healing inside of us, in our own blood. We need to accept God's dialysis of our souls and chose to accept His ongoing cleansing power that gives us the power to defeat our storms. When we are all alone, we can realize He is with us.

My biggest storm came when I was a single dad with an eight-year-old son and a terminally ill six-year-old daughter. She had been terminally ill for 5 years and her mother had left us. I felt all alone in my storm. That was the lowest point in my life. Many days I did not know how I made it through the daily rituals of making lunch, making it to work, grocery shopping and not to mention taking care of a bed bound daughter near the end stages of a horrible disease. I had to stay strong for my son and I eventually learned to find consolation in the eternal nature of God's word and His promises.

We all have pain that is our cross in life to bear. However, if you want to share in His glory, you have to bear your own cross. It is unique and different for each of us.

I also discovered a lifelong process of self-discovery by giving my pain to God in the form of Jesus work on the cross. I chose to believe God's love transfusion is meant just for me, and His blood cleansing is working in my body every day.

ঌ *CHILDHOOD PAIN* ঌ

When I was seven years old, I heard the story of God and His lamb's book of life. I was told that if I did not have my name in that book, I would go to hell and burn in the lake of fire. Well I definitely did not want that! It was a no brainer. With very limited exposure to scary movies, the only image I could conjure up was a fire set by Godzilla. She was in a firefight with another giant monster was getting barbecued. Besides the fear of hell, I wanted a commitment with Christ, God, or Jesus, whoever was in charge of my eternal destiny. Fear was only part of my young faith. I was also impressed with the fun and many examples of changed lives in my parents and their friends. The excitement was talked about in my family's social circles when someone was "saved." I noticed a big change with my dad. He stopped smoking, cussing, and treated the family much better. I heard and saw these stories throughout my childhood. I believed God would work on my behalf as well. As my faith took shape through my early years, God answered and saved me from various trials and problems. Did my fear of pain lead me to a saving knowledge of God or was I really just afraid of a spanking from God?

In my childhood, I received many spankings; some deserved and some probably not so much. I can remember hiding under the stairs hoping my dad would not find me if he thought I deserved a spanking. I thought, "out of sight, out of mind." Sometimes it worked and sometimes it did not. Is that how God hands out pain and storms in life as an adult? Are we all really just hiding under God's stairs? I prayed to God for relief from the spankings, seldom did the relief come as planned. There was no rhyme or reason, so I thought. I tried to be a good boy, but sometimes my curiosities got the best of me and I would get into trouble. I took sweets when I should not have: spanking. I did not listen to my mother: no spanking. Sometimes I got spankings for things I truly did not understand. I felt out of control. In my adult life, when trouble or storms happen, it takes me back to my childhood days hiding under the stairs from my father. Now as I gaze up at the clear night sky, I ponder to myself, half praying, "Father, am I hiding under your stars? Just waiting for the next spanking?"

What determines if a child gets spankings? As an adult I can now look back and see how it might have happened as well as how I dole out discipline in my house. Did I get more spankings when my dad was tired? Why didn't I get a spanking for disrespecting my mother? However, if I took dads candy bars, my butt was a goner! My dad always told us "This hurts me more than it hurts you" and "I'm doing this to make you a good boy." It did not seem so good for me at the time! I now realize the reasons depended on his character: my dad's view of justice, knowledge of our crimes, understanding of parenting, and his reasons to show discipline and love. God also gives spankings to show us He loves us.

God is a perfect and almighty Father and nothing prevents Him from disciplining His children. Therefore, He is all knowing, seeing, etc..... I can't get away with disrespecting my mother or anyone for that matter. When He punishes me, it is always for my good; it still does not feel good at the time. As a child I got away with some things that I should not have, but God sees it all, and nothing slips past Him. In addition,

along with His chastening His children, He is also merciful, gracious, and His love is perfect.

I am grateful for this part of His character. My earthly father did the best he could and I am grateful for the correction and love he gave very much. I am very proud of him, as he came from a broken home and did not have the advantage of good parent role modeling. As an adult, I am building on that awareness and want to apply Gods word and wisdom to understand the questions of life's spankings.

ঌ *HIDING UNDER THE STARS* ঌ

Then at the age of 11, when I did something that I knew I would normally get a spanking for and I did not get one. I thought, "I could have just got lucky, my dad did not feel like it." Then it did not happen again, and again. The spankings just stopped. Did God answer my prayer? I was now coming into a period of *Preparing in Peace.* My parents still gave me some discipline, but not by way of spankings anymore. God was working on my dad's heart. Now that the discipline of dad's spankings had ended, I was left to figure out how to discipline myself. Now I would go into the world and be handed over for Gods spankings. These are the painful things I call life's storms. They can be much worse than a red butt and we all need to prepare for them. When I was a child, I was thankful they stopped and gave God the credit for changing my dad's heart, but what was the bigger purpose and what did God want from me now?

With each storm in my adult life I realized nothing is hidden from God. He uses my storms for my good to teach me and ultimately leads to my blessings.

My human nature naturally drifts into hiding under the stairs **from God. He uses storms to get my attention and grow closer to him and his goodness.** What am I hiding from Him? Why do I try to hide? He sees and knows everything. I had many painful experiences in my pre-adult life that seemed to intensify the older I got and the stakes seemed to get bigger and bigger. Each storm I recovered from led me to a larger purpose and prepared me for the next testing storm of faith. God had prepared me to weather the storm of the death of my child. With each trial God worked on my behalf to provide my needs. In many times God was with me when it made more sense that I should have died. He must have had bigger plans for me. For each one of you reading this book, He has a reason for you to keep on living. What has God prepared you for?

All through my life God has been there, even when I faced more serious issues that many of us dread to ever face. Through my adult life, I faced various trials and pains where God showed himself to me in real tangible ways. I had a daughter die at the age of six that culminated from a long journey of being terminally ill for five years. These five years I lived in the eye of the storm, experiencing Gods sustaining power, even though death was all around me. Near the end of her life she was in pain and had very little signs of life. I depended on God and His people to help us take care of her. As she became a quadriplegic and then blind toward the end of life, death was a friend we are well acquainted with. She had many episodes where we thought she would die, but she did not. The night she did die, God made His presence known in a real and tangible way as she was ushered to heaven by the angels.

SIGNS OF FAITH

In the moment, we were not as aware how God gave us signs to show He was there. He is here, and He cares for me.

God cares for you and wants to show you His blessings in your storms if you will look to him in your hour of need.

Sometimes it is a tangible sign; sometimes it is just a sense of peace in my storm. How about you?

- Have you been where you thought that coincidence was maybe a sign from a greater power, or God?
- Was He trying to tell you something? I think we all have events and stories where God reaches into our human condition and sends us a sign. Do we see it as a sign from God if we are not looking? What does it mean?
- Does God really want to communicate with our little insignificant lives?
- Why did I have to go through the storm to see Gods hand of rescue? Sometimes He uses pain to get our attention.
- Why do bad things happen: chronic pain, and needless suffering?
- Can I avoid pain if I am serious about changing my life for the better?
- How can I use faith to find blessings in my storms?

In this book I unravel my findings from my journey of faith. I share my most painful experiences and how God led me on a journey to discover I was chosen to be blessed. He helped me to Prepare, Endure, and Restore blessings to me in the storms of my life. Yes, I know it sounds like the typical lemons to lemonade story, but my blessings would not have been possible if it had not been for my storms. These blessings are possible as I realize Gods true destiny for my life.

LETHAL DISCLAIMER

That's right lethal, not legal. Some things we will never understand until our bodies are dead! On the other side of the grave, in heaven, we will fully understand why we had the storms of life and why we go through so much to get blessings in life. Only God knows the full reason why pain and storms happen. I am thankful he has given me a glimpse of some of the reasons. I believe my book will help you find your blessings through my three secrets in the Faith Phases of

Prepare in Peace, *Endure the Eye*, and *Restore the Reason*.

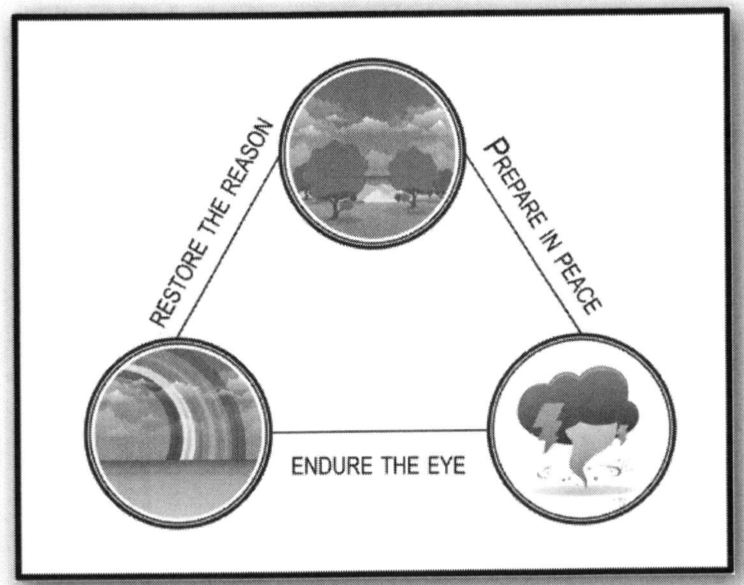

I will share them with you in this book in the hopes that you can see God has given you storms that can be transformed into blessings. My hope is that you will understand how God has uniquely chosen you to be blessed in the storms of your life. Despite, no, because of your storms, His intention is to use them for your good, your blessings! My goal is that you will see Gods messengers all around you that are trying to give you a Love Transfusion. In addition, God the Father is a perfect parent and knows what is best for you.

If you are looking through the spiritual lens of Gods word you can see the times that God used someone else as a Love Transfusion to believe the best in you that pick you up when you are at your lowest point.

You should also recognize looking to others for help is not enough. We have to look for healing and cleansing in our blood through Jesus in order to find our blessings uniquely planned for our lives. Then give God the credit and share your story of His healing as you give a Love Transfusions to others in their storms of life.

ঌ *YOU-DESIGNED BLESSINGS* ঌ

I have to remind myself God does not want us to hide under the stairs or anywhere under His stars, but relate with Him as a loving Father and not just a judge and punisher of our wrongs. He wants us to believe in Him that He is good and wants to restore what sin takes away. He also rewards His faithful.

After the death of my 1st daughter and my divorce, I thought I would never have a daughter or wife again. God showed me through faith and embracing His reason for my pain, He changed me and gave me a new life. That eventually led to getting remarried and having a stepdaughter, and then another daughter. God gave me signs of His blessings: My step-daughter was the same age as the one that died, and my second born daughter was born on the exact same date that my first daughter died.

Many see the storms in my life are just about disease, death, divorce, and daughters, but God used them all for my good and to bless me. My transformation only happened when I allowed His sovereign will to guide me. Only when we accept His soul healing in our storms can we see the blessings He has for us. In each of my faith shaking events I asked God to cleans my life, much like dialysis. His word cleansed me and other Christians shared God's Love Transfusion with me. This process gently guided me back on the rails of life to Gods plan and His blessings. I don't have all the answers, but just know that:

God uses our tragedies for His glory and our good. As you read this book see yourself and circumstances where He can speak to you and allow my story to transform your storms to blessings and challenge you to believe you are Chosen to be Blessed!

Secret 1

Prepare in Peace

Chapter 1

My Plans Don't Include Pain

He will wipe away every tear from their eyes, and death shall be no more, neither shall there be mourning, nor crying, nor pain anymore, for the former things have passed away.

REVELATION 21:4

❧ *REALITY IS REAL PAIN* ❧

"She has a rare genetic disorder, and the outlook is terminal and there is nothing we can do"

Said the geneticist at Detroit's Children's Hospital. The words burned in my brain as the Indian-speaking geneticist doctor counseled us in her office after the test results. We originally came in to hear why she was not able to stand without falling like a tree. We did not plan for THIS outcome. Nobody plans, or dreams of this nightmare.

"WAIT, my brain kept telling me, NOT MY DAUGHTER, this is supposed to happen to other people."

I begged God to get me out of the doctor's office; I wanted to wake up from this bad dream. I got my wish after a few more moments of medical jargon, sympathy, and

"...We'll see you on your next visit"

Came echoing down the hall. The reality of our daughter, Nicole Lynn Re was terminally ill came banging at the door of my logical mind. More like breaking into the plans of a normal predictable life. We had hopes and dreams planned out carefully since the minute she came out of the delivery room one year previously. This was the girl to match the 2-year-old brother, which matched with the cute ranch home we lived in, with a park in the backyard, 2 dogs, 2.5 cars, (I had a motorcycle I plan on fixing one day) and a boat.

All the pieces to our dream life fitted nicely, except this. I did not plan on this to happen; this was nowhere in my wildest expectations.

Her mother sat in the hospital lobby and I had my prayer answered to get out of the doctor's office quickly. I thought,

> *"if I can go out by myself for just a few minutes everything would be all right."*

As if I went outside, I could find a telephone booth to change into my superman outfit, and fix it, and then everything would be all right. Meaning, I could pray it away with my super powered God, that up until this point in my life had got me through many trials in life, but this one seemed too big. As I tried it, all my boggled brain could cry out was

"God Help!"

On my way to get the car, I literally pinched myself to see if this was just a really bad dream. "*Ouch! reality is painful,*" I murmured, as I pulled up to the hospital entrance to pick up my now doomed family. On the way home, it was very quiet. "I couldn't fix this one," I thought to myself. And as her mom glanced at me from the corner of her eye,

I thought to myself, *"God can't fix this one either,"* in that moment my faith felt broken.

This was not in my plans. Up until now, I always had the answer and God always delivered me in my distress. Even in the face of the surrounding challenges in my environment growing up in a rough neighborhood. I had a relatively easy life compared to many of my childhood friends. My parents were there for us; we had more than normal laughs and good times in my family and rarely were serious matters discussed, seriously! As a child that was fine with me, always looking for feel-good times and fun. All of the joking around and adolescent thrills never prepared me for facing death. How can you prepare for this? Nobody plans for his or her one-year-old baby to get a terminal prognosis. And now in my early 20's, all the laughs came to an abrupt halt. Up to this point I saw myself as in control of my plans and my life. My identity came crashing down to the ground, like tiny fragments of glass, sharp and painful. My paradigm had shifted and I felt like a victim. My worldview no longer worked and I felt the need to revise my plans. Now I needed to discover **who** I was in light of my new painful reality.

⚘ *IS MY LIFE PLANNED OR UNPLANNED?* ⚘

Understanding who I am better needs to be filtered through the eyes of my environment and what I think I am in control of, my plans. How could a loving God have plans like this for my life? Up to this point, all of my troubles and trials had ended up with some silver lining and God always came through for me - along with a little bit of my effort. That combination of God and my effort, our teamwork seem to be going fairly well up into this point, but how do I understand God now? Did He predestine my daughter to die as a child? How do my choices in life interact with Gods plans? Is it predestination or is it free will? As, I go through this book I will try to uncover both sides as 2 points of views: God and Mans perspective as I understand through my life's lens. I have come to believe my **life is a collaboration of both my free will plans and God's sovereign plans and He already knows the plans I will choose**.

In the book **The Harbinger** by Jonathan Cahn, he explains how God has a plan and we think we have a choice to choose his plan or choose our own plan, but it is actually both. Two men are in a rowboat having this discussion:

> "But that doesn't mean it wasn't planned" he added.
> "How could it be both?" I asked.
> "It takes two oars to make a boat go straight."
> "Meaning it's both free will and predestination?"
> "Meaning you need to use both oars and focus on keeping the boat straight so we can make it back to dry land."
> Excerpt from *The Harbinger*, Jonathan Cahn

I want to make it to the other side of my life to the reason God made me, but I can't do it without Gods sovereign plan and me choosing to follow it. I have plenty of ideas for my plans, but if I don't aggressively work to find

Gods plan I'll end up spinning in a circle in the middle of my life's stormy waters. It reminds me of the Israelites wandering I the desert for 40 years in search of the Promised Land. They could have taken about 1 month to get there, but because of their disbelief of Gods plan and discontentment, they never realized the dream God had planned for them. God let the non-grumbling believers possess the Promised Land. **In our controlling-our-own-lives mindset, we do not realize we are missing a blessing when we ignore God's plan.** Sometimes when things go "wrong" and we think somebody or someone is to blame for changing our lives plan.

Sometimes we wonder:

"Is changing the plan actually part of the plan?"

"Is pain part of God's plan?"

When I think about how God knew my daughter before she got sick and He assigned her to be terminally ill and then a slow fade to death. I think

"How? Why?"

My understanding and His are definitely different. Nevertheless, there I go again thinking just because God knows my plan and His plan; I have the faulty assumption that God considers these painful events and looks out for me by protecting me and keeping me from pain and harmful events like my daughter's illness. **If I look into God's word, I will know clearly that pain is actually part of God's plan and the fact that this evil disease did not come from him.** Just take for example Jesus and the pain he had to endure on the cross, He didn't want to, but he knew he had to. Jesus said

"not my will, but Thy will be done".

Jesus pain was part of the plan to save us. I think God has the same pattern in mind for you and me that he had for Jesus: My plan and His plan combine to defeat sin, evil, and death, (In this book I will refer to this as the storms of life).

Gods plan starts with our need to see ourselves the way God sees us, both the good and the bad. We are extremely loved by God and we are extremely doomed by sin. We are lost, fallen and hopelessly terminal.

WE ARE ALL TERMINALLY ILL

Dave Benton, a WCIA News anchor shared his story in a transparent way that he was battling brain cancer. On live TV, he announced his prognosis was bad, with only 6 months to live. The treatments did not work and the tumor had grown to the point of being inoperable. He also shared his faith and his heart on how he is thinking of others best interests. His main concerns were for him to do his job well, to serve his community, and viewers. He acknowledged there are others in the audience in his same condition and that was his concern as well. This self-less point of view that comes from his faith as a born again Christian and gives him peace, contentment, and assurance of his eternal home in the final stages of his life. We all admire his noble and strong approach to this storm in his life. Now, despite the prognosis, Benton says he is at peace and in God's hands.

> "*As you know, I'm a born again Christian,*" he said. "*I believe that I'm in God's hands. I'm at peace, and I know that He's going to take care of the days ahead and that the goal here is to have the best ones possible.*"

Let's examine Dave's outlook on this storm:

- Could it be that he sees who he is considering God's plan?
- An eternal perspective?

- Is it possible that Dave sees his storms how God sees them? *"not my will but thy will"*.
- How could a person have this peaceful attitude?
- How could someone approach the storm of death with an eternal perspective and considering others more important in this critical time of life?
- How will you be able to answer these questions when the storms turn in your direction?

For me, it was because I knew who God is and I sought him out. When I was in my storm in the lowest point in my life I faced my biggest test I've been training and God had prepared my faith so I could pass the test He prepared me for. Being prepared is the first step toward choosing your blessings in the storms of life.

God wants us to prepare in peace for the storms of life come that are sure to come so when they hit we'll be ready to allow God to transform them into blessings.

Up until age 23 I had sought God, study His Word, fellowship with his people, and got to know His character. This is not to say I was perfect at all, I had and continue to have the same struggles and challenges with my own sin and the evil all around us in this fallen world. Believe me, I'm by no means perfect; just ask those that know me. But what I've come to understand through the trials of my life is that He gives me the reason and purpose in Christ. When the storms of my life happen and I really need hope, I depend on him to help me through.

When tragedy entered my life with my daughter's illness and I was crying in my pain, I heard God's voice in the back of my head echoing:

> *"I will never leave you or for sake you."* (Deuteronomy 31:8)

From memory, words from the Gospels cried out to me in my pain when Jesus was denied:

> *"my God, my God why have you forsaken me."* (Matthew 27:46)

It makes perfect sense to know God's pain, is the only way I can share His blessings. I relate my pain in my daughter's death to what God went through. God allowed his son to go through death and pain for His ultimate glory. Why would I not expect my own cross to bear as well? After several other verses and remembrances of God's word flooded my mind when I had these sorrowful moments in my life, I came to the realization that this storm is God's plan for my life. I also know from faith, God's Word, and previous experience that He will make something good out of this tragedy. All of God's children have to experience storms in their life, because it is part of Gods plan and allows us to find our identity with the cross of Christ. In that way we share in the glory of God in the storms of our lives.

ঌ ANCHOR TO PREPARE FOR STORMS ঌ

Many times the plans we have or our expectations don't meet what we think God should deliver to us. These expectations cause an inward focus and contribute to becoming bitter, angry, and resentful. We all have expectations of what we should get out of life that are ingrained in our minds that we think we deserve and we plan on life to unfold as expected. Whether it is the family expectations of success and good hair, or images from TV that shape what we think we deserve out of life. We want things to go our way, by our plans, and our expectations. All it takes is one medium size storm to have that image shattered. Whether it is the pain of losing someone to a death, divorce, runaway, or the pain of serious illness that shrinks someone, we love down to a shadowy form of their health self. It always comes as a shock and a surprise that a tragedy happens to us. In our comfort and ease driven society of high tech marvels like video calls on our phones and high tech cars that park themselves for us, it is easy to believe we can avoid many of the painful storms of life that make us human.

When we embrace our humanity and humble ourselves to accept who we really are in God's plans. In His plan, we realize we are all terminally ill. In reality, we all need an "anchor" - in Christ! Can we be as brave as this terminally ill anchorman can? In the early days of Christianity, the symbol of an anchor gave Christians hope. Many anchor symbols were found in Christian dwelling caves of that era. As a child I sang the old hymn **The Solid Rock** I by Edward Mote (1797-1874) that references Hebrews 6:19:

"My anchor holds within the veil."

This is a phrase to meditate on and gives comfort to know Christ is your anchor and that He holds you up in the storm when everything else around you is swept away. All we have to do is follow Him to be spiritually prepared for a tragedy. If you are centered with Him in the normal everyday habits, then you will, by habit seek Him when the crisis hits you. In this way, God prepares you for the storms in life that are designed specifically for you to help you find Him in your storm. Like a lighthouse to lead you to safety, Gods word helps you understand the big picture and to endure when these horrible times hit your life.

PAIN FORCES YOU TO FIND GOD

As I faced the truth of my predicament of having a terminally ill 1-year-old baby, I felt I was on the edge of a nightmare roller coaster, just before you head down the first big hill. **In my mind I could hear the "click, click, click, click" of God's plan pulling me up to a place I did not want to go.** I thought,

> *"This is really happening and soon I will be dropped off the edge into my very strange unknown future with no way out."*

I felt unprepared and I definitely did not plan for it. In the pain of my daughter's disease, death, and the pain of our divorce: no amount of preparation could have prepared me for the pain I went through, because I did not want to go through it! However, I knew that God was in control and I remembered He has prepared for me when I felt I was not prepared to face my storms.

Do you sometimes feel as though you have the faith of a mustard seed?

Or even doubt His existence?

I definitely had my doubts as I went through some of my storms, but never denied God altogether, rather I cried out to Him Aba, Father! He made a miracle of the little faith and preparation I did have. Just like Jesus feeding the thousands with the one little boy's lunch, at times my faith felt like the little boys, inadequate for God's plan ahead. I prayed, languished, and sometimes even wrestled in anger with God over my plan vs. His plan. Even though I prepare for my life of faith according to my plans. Like the little boy, he only planned to feed just himself, but God had bigger plans.

**My small faith was barely enough for me,
but God's plan is to multiply my faith and is endless in eternity.
He wants to feed thousands with from my small faith.
His message of faith from my life's story is always bigger than my plans.**

What about you?

What painful storms have you gone through and have you seen why God changed your plans?

He wants you to see He has a plan to prosper you bigger than you can see. Looking back on it now, I'm not sure what I expected, that life would go along without any tragedies indefinitely. Perhaps I was just childish in my faith, far from a childlike faith: believing that all things are possible with God and trusting unconditionally. Ultimately, I knew that my source of comfort would be found in God's word and His people.

ꕥ *ROOTS HOLD YOU DOWN IN THE STORM* ꕥ

My pastor, Jeff Stimpson, recently discussed the need for building strong community in the church. He said it was much like the roots built in the mighty sequoia tree. It grows up to 250 feet high and 30 feet wide but has roots only three feet deep. Despite the shallow depth it withstands the strongest of storms. This is possible because of the wide network of roots it is connected to that spans 300 feet in diameter. This connected-ness allows the tree to be strong just like we should be connected to the body of Christ to conquer our storms.
You might ask yourself:

> "In my pain, how did I know that God would be there to comfort me and bring back scripture references to my remembrances?"

It was because of my strong spiritual roots that developed over many years that prepared me. It all started with my experiences that made up my worldview. My history and knowledge of God and His saving power came early at 7 years old. It wasn't just the message that the preacher delivered that spoke to my heart:

it was Gods people, my parents,
and changed lives that impacted me.
We sang songs about the
"Family of God"
and we really felt it.

Both of my parents came from broken homes and destructive environments. We didn't have much extended family to rely on. We wanted a bigger family to belong to. Many of the people in the church treated us like family. They showered love on my siblings, my parents, and me by praying with us, fellowshipping with us, and most importantly eating in each other's homes and becoming our friends. It's a lot to ask of a couple to invite the family I grew up with into their home. Including me there was five of us rambunctious kids, and we usually broke something! The lives of my parents and friends spoke volumes as we saw changes in my parent's lives; I wanted some of that happiness and power to overcome problems in my life.

My parents became involved in the church and started serving and giving back. My dad helped where we could and my mom taught Sunday school classes and bible quizzing. The three of us boys, myself and my two brothers were involved in bible quizzing with our mom as the coach. The first year we were in it, we went to quizzing competitions around Southeast Michigan competing for scholarships and trophies with other churches in the region. We had to study the bible, because our mom was the coach. More importantly in these peaceful years, God was connecting my spiritual roots with my family, friends, the church, and knowledge of Gods word.

HOW HIGH? FAITH THAT JUMPS

My mother was the spiritual warrior for the family. As such, she nagged us every day to study God's word and the quizzing materials. Of course, we would rather watch another rerun of *Gilligan's Island*. I wanted to do well, compete, and do something good for God. I thought,

"Maybe God will give me an extra nice mansion in Heaven."

The quiz competitions worked on a buzzer system, where the sensor was placed on the bottom of the chairs. Whoever lifted their bottom off their chair first, their light and a buzzer would turn on. You would then have to answer the question. I studied the materials from 1st and 2nd Corinthians that year very diligently and was excited to compete. I prepared by tape-recording the verses and listened to them under my pillow at night. However, when the time came for the competition events, our team lost every event.

We felt like the *Bad News Bears*, losing all the time with very little points. My dad usually drove the church van and made it a family outing, along with the other quiz team members. My family always had a great time win or lose.

However, I was getting tired of always losing and I didn't understand why it had to be that way. In my family's view, we were prepared to be losers because we were more focused on fun. We were also accustomed to trash talking our abilities and ourselves because it was more fun. At the next very important district quiz meet where a scholarship was on the line, I sat there on my buzzer and prayed earnestly to God,

> *"God, if you are real, please help me win this quiz meet. I know this is your will and I studied your word, now help others see that I have studied your word and how important it is, help my weak faith and help me to win!"*

I really wanted to show how hard I had study and I wanted to do something good for God so that He would get the glory. As soon as I prayed, I felt empowered, alive and knew that God would help me. The quizmaster started asking a question and I recalled the answer I studied, it just clicked. I jumped up from my seat and the buzzer and light on my chair went off. To my surprise, the quizmaster called my number. I walked up to the microphone, finished the question, and then gave the answer. As I walked away, I heard the voice from the judges' table say, "correct." When I sat back down my teammates all gave me high five's! We were all excited to not have a goose egg. I prayed to myself before they called the next question, thanking God for what a wonderful thing He did giving me the power and confidence. The next question came up and again I stood up first, answered and got it correct again. I kept on jumping up first and answering correctly.

My winning ways were inspiring others on my team and they got some questions correct too. By the time the contest was over, I had won the first place award and my team won the overall first place award. Afterward, all the teams were shocked and surprised. We had never won any competition in the past two years and were supposed to lose. Some even complained that we took too many points and made others feel bad. Just goes to show that whenever God blesses you, some people will complain for your victory.

Be prepared for resistance from people not in God's Plan when you start to get onboard with Him, Some people will always be jealous when you win with God's answered prayers!

When it came time to get the trophies and awards, I gave God all the credit. Looking back on it now, I know that this quiz meet was more about building my faith in His word to prepare me for His plans than winning a nice plastic trophy and an award.

ঌ *FAITH'S LIFE'S CYCLE* ঌ

I'm not sure why God blessed me with winning this award and trophy, but I believe it's from obedience investment of faith that God delivers a fruit of promise. I call this process **Faith's Life's Cycle**. As I have gone on my journey, I've noticed that if I just obey what God is asking me to do in my life, He will provide direction and His will when the time is right and bless me in the process. Faith's lifecycle goes like this: **L**ost, **I**n a storm, **F**ound, **E**ternal perspective, and **S**ave. (L. I. F. E. S.) There is an understanding of my condition to see God blessing me and being there for me when I call out to him in the storm. I was:

- **L**) Lost in my faith, doubting if God was real,
- **I**) In a storm of Insecurity and Self-Pity Identity,
- **F**) Found when I took steps of action and wrestling with God in prayer,
- **E**) Eternal Perspective was gained when I uncovered Gods purpose for pain in His Word.
- **S**) Save the memory for the next phase of God's plan.

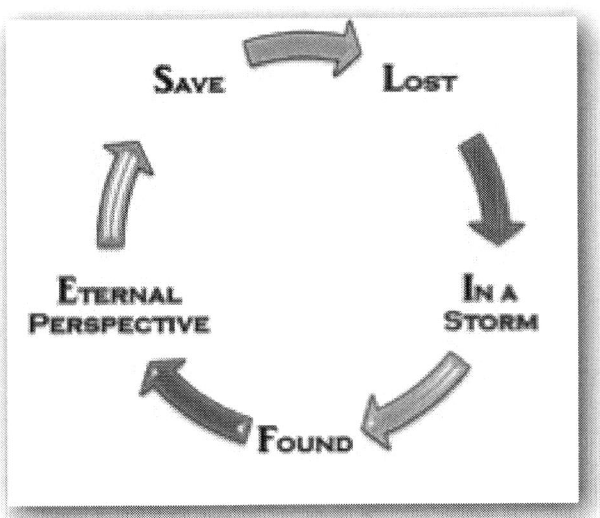

It does not mean that I can operate God like a candy machine. However, it does mean if I do my part, God is faithful and will deliver me in some way if I put my faith in him. It all starts with preparing in peace for a relationship with him, understanding that I am chosen to be blessed, but in order to receive these blessings I have my part to play in God's plan. He wants a bigger harvest in my life than I can plan or imagine.

ঌ *SEEDS OF FAITH GROW INTO BLESSINGS* ঌ

The fruit of God's promise starts with the seed of faith based in my relationship with God the Father. Our seeds need care and nurturing. In the book of Genesis, chapter 15 God promises to bless and multiply Abraham. He told him his offspring would be as many as the stars in the sky and the grains of sand on the beach. God had a plan, but Abraham struggled with following it. He made many mistakes because of a lack of faith and following his own plans. After many painful storms, he finally ended up obeying God. Then God gave real, tangible blessings he could see. At one point Abraham was willing to sacrifice his son's life, now that is faith in action! Abraham went from very little faith to great faith that led to blessings. All along God kept inserting His plan into Abraham's life to deliver fruit from His promise. His promises are in his word for us to look to and understand whom God is. This is part of **preparing in times of**

peace that is pivotal before you are in a storm, a crisis of faith, and looking for direction. The seeds of faith are from God's word to prepare us for life's storms. If we don't take care of His promises by reading, meditating and take actions of faith that show we believe in those seeds, then nothing will grow and our faith is dead.

If we believe in God's promises, like seeds of faith, then there are things we will do. We will live a life of action in accordance with the fruit we are expecting to produce in our lives.

Just like God's promises to Abraham, they were not necessarily just for him. This mighty nation that would cover the whole earth he couldn't see it right then, but he had to take actions of faith that eventually led to God's blessings. God's plans are there for us to follow and may be painful at times but He is teaching us to trust and know Him better. God may only give us sight for one-step at a time, but in order to nurture our seeds of faith that will lead to blessings, we must accept His sovereignty and put our lives under his command.

Chapter 2

Faith in Life and Death

That is all faith requires, having the faith to keep on trying. It is a life-long practice to see what is unseen.

Ronald David Re

BULLETS AND BIBLES

The Seceder Presbyterians came from Scotland to gain freedom, religious and otherwise. The English Crown persecuted them because of their quest for freedom and their outspoken opposition to slavery. Reverend James Wallace from the Seceder Presbyterians was a famous opponent against slavery that founded the New California Church in Jerome Township Ohio. This site is just a few miles from my current residence in Delaware Ohio. The story goes on to tell how President Abraham Lincoln made the call to war to defend our union against slavery. Shortly after Lincoln's address to the nation on April 24th, 1861 bullets and a Bible laid on the Pulpit of the new California church as Sunday morning services were about to begin.

The preacher at that time was The Reverend B.D. Evans. He preached a patriotic message, summoning men to action while the bullets and the Bible laid between the preacher and the congregation as a call to action. That day 40 men came forward to enlist in the Union army to defend what they believed in. By the time the Civil War ended, in all 367 men from Jerome Township served in the fight for freedom and racial equality. This was one of the highest volunteer rates in the country and the war killed 17 of these men. They are buried in the little white churches' cemetery as a reminder to act on what YOU BELIEVE IN!

What kind of belief does it take to be willing to die for a cause you believe in? I believe their faith prepared them to live their life for a purpose higher than just their own needs. The New California Church in Jerome is a sign for all to remember - your beliefs dictate your actions, even to the point of death.

Freedom is a costly belief that many have died for and an even bigger idea to live for. The belief of the Bible led many to pickup bullets, bullets of action!

These men used the bible to determine their faith and acted on their belief with bullets. What have you had to sacrifice because of your belief? Many in America have not had to sacrifice much because of the sacrifice of the few that defend our freedoms. This season of peace allows one to prepare for storms that will ultimately come into everyone's life. I challenge you to live for a higher calling of faith – to find your bullets. In this way,

the bullets of action prepare you for the storms yet to come and enable you to live with a passion, because you found your purpose.

We will dive more into your purpose when we look at *Restoring the Reason* in Secret 3 of this book. These stories of faith in action only come by centering your world on God's Word and depending on the work of the cross that guides your journey. This symbol below represents a life that has God's word as the source for all decisions, considering the example that Jesus gave. He said, and I paraphrase

> "All of God's Laws are summed into these two commands - Love God with all your heart and love your neighbor as yourself." (Luke 10:27)

Freedom is a costly belief that many have died for and even bigger idea to live for. The belief of the Bible led to bullets, bullets of action! When you find your passion and belief, live your life as bullets for Gods kingdom.

☙ *ELECTRIC FAITH THAT CONQUERS FEAR* ☙

At 17 years old my best friend Kenny and I were up in a tree goofing around after school. We told my mom we were "studying", but we had a pair of binoculars, hoping to see something we should not be looking at. There was nothing to see but we were curious. Probably too curious! As we were competitive, we both climbed higher in our part of the tree to see who could get the highest. As I was looking around the different backyard windows, I felt the tree vibrate. I called out to my friend, "Kenny, what's that?" he did not respond after a couple more times, but my eyes were glued to the spectacles. After a few seconds longer than I expected without any response, I looked away from the binoculars to see my friend frozen like a statue and making a wheezing sound. He tried to speak and faintly I could hear the words

"h……e…….l………p,"

as he helplessly breathed out in a barely audible tone. His hand was stuck to a large electric wire that ran through the branches about 25 feet in the air. Panic instantly set in as I realized what was happening with the feelings of the electrified vibrating tree. I knew I had only moments to act if my friend would live or die!

In that moment of life or death, it appeared life stood still as my mind thought about my beliefs - in what I knew was true about electricity and eternal life. Electricity had principals that could save me, and so did my belief in Jesus.

I wanted both of us to go to heaven, but not now! I jumped down. Really, I shimmied down the rough bark of the tree, scraping my hands and chest along the way down to the ground. I ran for my life, away from the electrified tree in fight or flight mode.

"Finally on the solid ground of the earth,"

I thought, but really far from solid ground as I had a decision to make.

Run to safety or go to the tree and risk my life?

I knew in that moment those were the only two choices I had, as I paused from running to my back door. In those few seconds I prayed and asked God for guidance, but I knew my choices:

I was half way between the safety of the answers of others and the tree of fear and faith.

I knew I had to decide now if I wanted to save my friend's life. If I waited to go get help, I would be attending his funeral.

My love for my friend pushed me back in the direction of the tree.

My faith and belief helped me decide to take actions of faith, (those are my bullets). Even in my fear, I had to try. In those seconds of indecision my actions were guided by my beliefs and love. I ran to the base of the tree climbed up about 16 ft. where I could just grab my friend's foot and I pulled with all my strength. A second later he came crashing into my arms as his limp body folded with the weight of gravity.

He was freed with just my touch.

He was aware and conscious, but very sore. He spent a few days in the hospital to be monitored, but he was alive and would be fine. I wonder if this is what Jesus felt? The decision to go to the cross took faith in the face of great fear. In spite of the fear, He chose to die.

His love for us pushed Him in the direction of the tree.

I can't imagine the anguish. Nevertheless, we all have a choice to go in the direction of the tree to save our friends. We all have an opportunity to show them the tree of the cross by the decisions we make in life.

Does your life point to faith and a relationship with God our creator?

In our moment of life or death, we all stand half way between the safety of others to save us or in the answers at the tree.

If we choose to keep it safe, we can go to the safety of our home and the opinions of others in our lives. Our eternal destiny depends on what we think and know to be true about this life and eternal life. Our beliefs teach us principals that save us, a belief in Jesus.

We are freed with just Jesus's touch

from the grip of sin to believe and have faith that conquers fear. I'm glad I freed my friend from the tree, but more importantly I'm glad Jesus went to His tree to free all that will believe.

ꟸ JESUS AND GEORGE - MEDICINE AND FAITH ꟸ

Many of the great men and women in history lived with an awareness of their reason in life because they were prepared for greatness when the time was right. Two such heroes' in my life are George Washington and Jesus Christ. In many ways, they prepared for their moment of greatness to live out their purpose. They both had faith in God to fulfill their mission. Not only that, many others that started our country had a Christian faith. Most all of the signers of the Declaration of Independence were dedicated Christians. Much like **Patrick Henry**, a voice of the country said during turbulent times:

> "An appeal to arms and the God of hosts is all that is left us. But we shall not fight our battle alone. There is a just God that presides over the destinies of nations. The battle, sir, is not to the strong alone. Is life so dear or peace so sweet as to be purchased at the price of chains and slavery? Forbid it almighty God. I know not what course others may take, but as for me, **give me liberty, or give me death."** (Patrick Henry)

They preached the gospel of Jesus Christ and believed in the biblical principle that set us free from sin and death. **Your belief predicts your reality**. These patriots believed Gods word.

The belief in the cause of freedom led patriots to action that risked their lives; it is also true for followers of Jesus and His cause of salvation.

Many Christians throughout history, before and after Christ was born have sacrificed their lives for the belief that Heaven is real and Jesus conquered death on the cross. This should cause us to live a life where we have hope that death is not the end. This should encourage us to live in a way that honors God in the storm of death.

I believe George Washington was the first president of the United States, over 200 years ago: I see the proof of his life in the reality I see all around me with the nation he fought to create, The United States of America. I believe in the principals of America, so you might call me patriotic. I took actions to put my life at risk by joining the Army, just as my two brothers also served in the armed forces. My belief led to actions in my life. It does not mean Americans, patriots, or soldiers are perfect in their belief, but it does mean they will let their belief direct their actions. In some way we all show what kind of soldiers we are by the actions we take that support the beliefs we have by faith. The storms of life test your true colors of faith and show what uniform you wear.

As it is true with Jesus, I believe He existed over 2000 years ago with a life of miracles, death, and resurrection that founded the salvation nation. This is a nation without borders and whose citizens choose to believe in him and will live in heaven for eternity. Salvation causes those that believe in His principles to sacrifice their lives and live for Jesus. I'm not talking about Christianity you and I hear about as a formal religion you hear in newspapers and scandalous tabloids. I'm talking about a personal relationship following Jesus. If you could for just a moment, skip over the scandalous stories and hypocrisy of mere humans like myself, that try to follow Jesus principles, you will find a glimmer of hope for humanity.

All it takes to be a Christ follower is faith, one-step at a time, to believe in the Good News of Christ.

Just look at the evidence of Jesus followers that died rather than denouncing Him. What would the heart of a cynic really think? Any logical mind would have to conclude He is as real as George Washington. Not only the historical evidence in human lives throughout history, but also the examples of changed and sacrificed lives. There is also further evidence of freedom gained by those that try to practice His principles.

That is right, - just try faith!

It is not perfect but all believers are practicing faith until we get to heaven and become perfect, just like the practice of medicine. Many doctors are not perfect or completely accurate in their prognosis and treatment. We do not call them hypocrites because they keep on trying.

That is all faith requires, having faith to keep on trying. It is a lifelong practice to see what is unseen

to gain eternal life. The practice of faith and medicine are both high callings – worth the effort!

ೋ *IN THE STORM – HE'S IN THE LUGGAGE* ೋ

We carry around the emotional failures and successes into our storms. Ou**r life's storms high's and low'**s frame our view of God. These spiritual memories are the emotional baggage we take with us as we weather subsequent storms.

Each experience adds or subtracts from our faith in God. How you handle your emotional baggage in your storms is a secret to *preparing in peace.*

If we filter our emotions through Gods Word, then we have the right luggage to help us through the storm. Our emotional life seen as **L.U.G.G.A.G.E** are as follows:

- **L**ove God first.
- **U**nderstand He has a different goal in my pain.
- **G**ive God the credit for my success and blessings in life.
- **G**od's Word gives me wisdom.
- **A**ttitude of gratitude toward God in all things.

- **G**o where He leads me, trusting in faith.
- **E**motional control to find His direction.

When I consider my spiritual life as LUGGAGE, it helps me when going through a storm. I need to realize God is there as long as I open my suitcase and use what He has given me. Here are some examples of carrying God with me as my *luggage* in my storms:

- **L**ove God first: But I do not always recognize him in my pain because I'm too busy dwelling on myself and my problems.
- **U**nderstand He has a different goal in my pain: It is only when I look to God and His ways that I find comfort, meaning, and value in my suffering and the suffering of those around me. I could recognize my suffering and those around me was the same of that of our dear savior Jesus.
- **G**ive God the credit for my success and blessings in life: I also remember in times of doubt when God delivered me in the past and when He's been there for me.
- **G**od's Word gives me wisdom: If I'm wise enough I will sense God's Spirit or prompting and I'm able to think of my spiritual answers to the storms of life. Then I am able to go to my heavenly father and seek his counsel in wisdom. I did not go there as much as I should, but eventually I work my way around to seeking His face, His will, and His solace.
- **A**ttitude toward God is everything. I realized in my own spiritual history that when I seek God the most is when I prepared my heart to be close to him before the storm approaches. I am also more prone to seek his will and direction and comfort when I am in a storm where I see no way out except depending on him.
- **G**o where He leads me: Many times when I'm in a spiritually in tune frame of mind God shows me signs or brings to my remembrances what he would have me do in my trial.
- **E**motional control to find His direction: I learned to not trust my emotions and look to God to do the right things, even if my heart

> was not in it. By following God in faith, I learned obedience was better than feeling good about my storm. This attitude of an obedient soldier allowed me to find direction in my storms.

I have my moments of doubt and wonder where God is. When I get lost in the storm I check what I have in my luggage of life and find what is missing. I sometimes do not have the right things packed. I realize I need to go back and pack the things I am missing to get through the storm. This means going to Gods word to translate my hurt and pain to see what God says about my storm. With the right things firmly attached to the luggage rack of my life, I find his signs to point the way.

WHO SHOULD FEAR DEATH?

Many times, we think of blessings and God's favor we think of prosperity, possessions, and wealth. However, we know that life is full of many other blessings besides what money can buy. We should be careful to think of God's blessings in our spiritual well-being before we think of our physical well-being. It is often spoke of in the Bible that our spiritual well-being is more important. Who should we trust in this life and for salvation for the next life? Psalm 49 speaks about this dilemma of whom we put our trust in or better yet, what we put our trust in.

Let us examine Psalm 49 from the NIV version:

> "Hear this, all you people; listen, all who live in this world,
> My mouth will speak words of wisdom; the meditation of my heart will give you understanding. I will turn my ear to a proverb; with the harp I will expound my riddle: Why should I fear when evil days come, when wicked deceivers surround me— those who trust in their wealth and boast of their great riches? For all can see that the wise die, that *the foolish and the senseless also perish, leaving their wealth to others*......People, despite their wealth, do not endure; they are like the beasts that perish. This is the fate of those who trust in themselves, and of their followers, who approve their sayings. They are like sheep and are destined to

> die.... But God will redeem me from the realm of the dead; he will surely take me to himself. Do not be overawed when others grow rich, when the splendor of their houses increases; for they will take nothing with them when they die, their splendor will not descend with them. Though while they live they count themselves blessed— and people praise you when you prosper— they will join those who have gone before them, who will never again see the light of life......." (Psalm 49:1, 3-20 NIV)

We can see that God's view of life and death levels the playing field for both rich and poor. It's all about whom one puts their trust in. From **Matthew Henry's Concise Commentary,** the only thing that provides peace when facing death is if you have God with you. He has the following comments on Psalm 49:

> "We seldom meet with a more solemn introduction: there is no truth of greater importance. Let all hear this with application to ourselves. The poor are in danger from undue desire toward the wealth of the world, as rich people from undue delight in it."

The poor get trapped in desire for riches while the rich get trapped with the delighting in riches.

It seems to me that if you are too rich or too poor you may have temptation to pursue wealth as a God. Whatever you pursue as your most important delight or desire becomes what you put your trust in when you face a storm of life, including the most perilous - the storm of death. **Matthew Henry's Concise Commentary** then going on to express the security that one finds in Christ while facing death:

> "The psalmist begins with applying it to himself, and that is the right method in which to treat of Divine things. Before he sets down

> the folly of carnal security, he lays down, from his own experience, the benefit, and comfort of a holy, gracious security, which they enjoy who trust in God, and not in their worldly wealth. In the Day of Judgment, the iniquity of our heels, or of our steps, our past sins, will compass us. In those days, worldly, wicked people will be afraid; but wherefore should a man fear death who has God with him?"

Our society is not that different throughout the ages: striving to prolong and enhance human life. It is very costly and extensive endeavor. Whether one is rich or poor, we all want the same thing. As we can see from the text above, where we put our security determines how we will pursue our life's goals. Health, diet, and the physical care of our bodies and lives should not prioritize above our spiritual well-being. All it takes is a storm of life, trauma, or some painful experience to change our priorities to question our eternal existence.

~ *What are you putting your trust in*?
~ *What is your most important delight*?

❧ *THE ANGRY AND HOPELESS* ❧

If we believe in God's word, then we grieve differently in death. With the acknowledgement of the eternal God, you recognize He is in control of our eternal destination. In the song by *Casting Crowns*, **Praise you in this Storm**:

> "I would have thought by now, you'd have stepped in and save the day... ... I praise the God who gives and takes away... You never left my side"

You see the heart cry of a Christ follower that recognizes our hope lies not in the temporal joys this side of the grave. We know from our faith

"To die is to gain heaven ... and to live is for Christ." (Phil 1:21)

This means we have a win – win attitude to lean on when times are tough because there is a hidden plan in the pain life sends our way.

Only by looking back at previous pains and how God used those situations for our good can we realize God's strategy to grow us up and give us ultimate peace, joy, and His blessings.

A number of years ago at an upscale hotel in Philadelphia, I sat in a silent meeting room with about 30 men waiting to ease their troubled minds. We were at a yearly *National Tay-Sachs and Allied Disease,* (NTSAD) conference. This non- profit was very helpful in the care and counseling for my family to get through the daily issues with having a terminal ill child with a similar classification of diseases. They had a breakout session for fathers to share their feelings with a licensed physiologist. Most of the fathers in the group had two different outlooks on what they were going through.

The first group had an attitude of fatalism: that nothing they did in their life mattered and God was a cruel game master handing out diseases, deformity, and pain at will and their children were in the crosshairs. Their anger hid their fears. This told me they had a lack of faith and knowledge of the sovereignty of God.

The few that spoke up had deep anger that veiled a sense of entitlement, pride, and conceit of life. They expected something – the ideal life, a storybook life free of random pain and sadness.

But that is not the truth of our terminal condition and this storm is sent as a message to save them for eternal life.

The second group of men barely spoke at all and had their emotions bottled up. I took this as a sign of denial and defiance. In their pain, they turned to stone. Their faces said what they could not – defeat.

They did not have the will to be angry anymore, but just accepted their lives and families were doomed with a look of hopelessness.

This was a concentrated group of sadness that I wanted to share hope with.

I shared my spiritual view of our plight with both these groups: **the angry and the hopeless.** I had been in both groups at different times, but did not stay there thanks to the Holy Spirit renewing my mind and having an eternal perspective of my storm. My view was only different because of the hope and attitude change that God's word provides. My hope was real, but sometimes my emotional pain overpowered my life and doubt crept in.

We all bring our experience to bear on what we expect out of life. If you have an easy crisis free childhood, like myself then you expect an easy going, trouble free life as you grow into your adult years. When we are young and especially in our teenage years and young adult phase of life we feel we can conquer the world. If this is you, then you know the invincible feeling that you can do whatever you put your mind to. Then, as we attempt to live out our dreams, we hit roadblocks: It could be other people, our own view of ourselves, tragedy, illness, stuff. Just like the saying, "Stuff happens." Then we have derailed dreams, and the once invincible ideas of young adulthood come crashing down around us. We have our reality bubble pop! As we try and fail, and continue the cycle of "stuff happening" to us our dreams begin to slowly fade into the background while we just struggle to survive in reality. The process of losing one's dreams, not achieving one's goals, and the reality of the human condition causes us to question one's faith. We ask ourselves, "Is God really there with me in my mess? Does He have good plans for my life?"

ꕥ *SAYING GOOD BYE* ꕥ

One night at a Bible study, I was asked,

> *"What was the time you felt God speak to you the most or influenced your life the most?"*

I was reluctant to speak about this because I thought it might be prideful of me and seem like bragging.

Just then, I realized the events of my life were true and were not about me. They were how great God is and he was using my life to tell his–story.

I needed to share them for the glory of God and it might help others. I shared the story of the night my first daughter, Nicole, died.

On a normal Wednesday evening, I would get the kids ready and we would go to church. I would help teach bible verses. Nicole would go to the childcare. And our son would go to the kid's program called *"AWANA" (Approved Workmen Are Not Ashamed.)* The past few weeks Nicole had become too sick to go with us. Several family members, Nurses, and Friends were over our home due to her serious turn for the worse. A cadre of visitors to our home had become routine procedure over the past couple of years. They had a sense of urgency and that she would die at every episode. I was the eternal optimist; that God is in control and never panicked the 10 or more times, it got "serious."

Gods spirit prompted me that this time was different and to be more aware that night. That day had not gone well for my now 6-year-old terminally ill daughter, Nicole. She was now in 24-hour hospice care in our home. Her breathing was shallow and her vitals were low. We were all scrambling around to take the next steps, whatever that was. Looking back on that night now feels horribly ironic. Like an expectant parent and the birth of their first child and all of the nervous hustle and bustle. We had been expecting this for 3 years or so, but you are never ready to say goodbye to your baby.

I am not sure if I was just being stubborn or just wanted my way, but I always felt that we should try to live a normal life as possible for our 8-year-old son, Zachary. I was determined to get him to church for his kid's program. I believe the Holy Spirit told me this time was different, but I should be at church. It was a walk–by–faith moment. I should be at home with my sick child, but God told me to go to church anyway. I felt like Abraham going to sacrifice his son. He had no sacrifice but his child, and went to sacrifice anyway, even though it felt wrong. So off to church I went.

She was very sick and the healthcare workers blocked my car in the driveway. I did not want to disturb them in their care for my daughter, but I was going to church! As events transpired, a different health worker was leaving our home, so my son and I bummed a ride to church, knowing I could get a ride home from our friends. Upon arriving at church, I was met by the wife of our closest friends, Jeanne. (God also planned for her to be a Registered Nurse). I informed her of the situations back home and she validated my feelings of tonight being the night for Nicole's passing. She offered to do anything she could and would come over after church to help take care of her.

We proceeded calmly in the usual prayer meeting, and then I needed a ride home. I am ever so grateful for *Pastor Ronald Graef*, the lead pastor and his wife felt the spirits call to accompany me home. They were spiritually alert to the Lords will and drove me home. I thought

> *"what an opportunity, to see if he could come in and comfort all of us on this eventful night."*

I knew something would happen, so I asked them to come in and give us assurance of where my daughter would go when she died. I also thought this would be a way Nicole's dying could be a way to minister and witness to the group of workers at the house.

Our humble pastor had a golden opportunity holding our baby in a living room full of people. He discussed heavens streets of gold, Jesus love, and our daughter's soon to be heavenly home.

In that moment I knew why I had gone to church, God provided the reason in pastor Greaf.

The pastor had given us assurance and a wonderful prayer for Nicole and our troubled family. I was completely under Gods direction that night as I felt God prompting me to take the family away from the crowded living room. I asked the caregivers and visitors to give us some time alone with our daughter in her bedroom. My thoughts flashed back to how God ordained our purchase of the home five years ago because her bedroom was perfectly decorated for a girl. Her bedroom was still the same as when we moved in: a circus themed wallpaper, toys, animal knickknacks, and stuffed animals on the walls. As we entered, the room, I mourned for the life never lived in that room. Rarely had the four of us been in that room for a purpose of fun and silliness. Now we would be together for the last time as a family – to say goodbye. We all said a little prayer ushering her off to heaven. I explained to Zachary in child-like words why we were in the room together, sensing the urgency. He said a simple prayer like this:

"I love you Nicole, have fun in heaven running around."

Since she had never been able to walk, I thought this was his great faith. Her mom said a quick prayer showing her love and then I let her know she would be going to heaven soon and it was ok to go now, and how much we all loved her and will see her again one day. I also let her know that she would be healthy and whole in heaven and this would be a great day for her in heaven.

The care workers left. Then our best friends Larry and Jeanne took actions of love: Larry took our son to my parents for the night and Jeanne offered to relieve the Hospice workers and to stay overnight with her so we parents could get some much needed sleep. My ex-wife and I cried ourselves to sleep that night mourning for many things. I was mourning the end of our marriage and horrible disease that took our daughter. I was thankful, she stayed with me that night. Around 4AM the next morning, we heard a knock on the bedroom door. It was Jeanne our good friend with tears in her throat she announced gently through a partially opened door:

> *"She went home to be with Jesus."*

Jeanne called the nurses back again and took care of any legalities. Her mom and I were just in shock, but at the same time somewhat relieved. I knew she was in a better place and her suffering from the five years of illness had ended. I was thanking God for endurance and guiding me that night.

ঌ *PREPARE FOR TOTAL SURRENDER* ঌ

Her sufferings are a constant reminder to me of the sufferings of Christ and the promise He keeps for those whose trust is in Him. That night I witnessed the love of God and His family with the pastor's counsel and the Christian friends acts of faith. They showed true piety of faith in action that displays Gods heart. In Colossians, 3:17 we see Gods plan includes our actions of surrender to His will:

> "And whatever you do, whether in word or deed, do it all in the name of the Lord Jesus, giving thanks to God the Father through him." (Colossians 3:17 NIV)

My friends were the heroes in this night and God received the Glory. Now their actions are part of my story. What acts of God can you think of that might be part of someone else's story?

Any time you reach out to others in faith to share Gods love in some action, word or deed, God will use it to restore another's heart.

It will help them heal and restore the reason He has you in their life's storm. I am so glad these dear friends were:

- Spiritually mature,
- Prepare to minister and
- Most importantly acted on Gods prompting.

This is where God lives in the praises of His people.

Your life can praise him by the things that you do to show love to others.

In the moment, they surrendered to the will of God. Larry and Jeanne had plenty of excuses they could have used. They had jobs and three children to take care of, but they dropped everything to obey Gods will. I pray to be like that! That also gives life so much purpose and reason that is bigger than the world we see.

Thank you Larry, Jeanne, and Pastor Graef

Most importantly, Thank you Jesus!

Chapter 3

Grace for Girls in the Signs that Save

"Unless you people see signs and wonders," Jesus told him, "you will never believe."

John 4:48

ꕥ *SAYING DADDY* ꕥ

She progressed to the point of eating cheerios, babbling, and walking along furniture. I soon was hopeful for her saying those precious words "Daddy!" Then, we noticed some problems that were difficult to understand. When she was one years old she stopped making her growth milestones and cried more than normal. She would pull up to the couch, loose her balance, and then fell back like a tree. Alas, we started the process of visiting doctors and discovering her fate. Ends up she had a rare genetic brain disorder called *GM1 gangliosidosis*. This very sad disease made me question God. I settled for smaller prayers and just getting through each day one by one. After the prayers for my daughter came back with the answer of "no," and the disease progressed, my requests of God became less demanding. I thought,

> *"If God is not going to heal her, maybe I can ask for something less audacious."*

Accepting Him not healing my daughter was difficult, but now I started to doubt God. Is He here in my misery? Are the nay-sayers of God right? At times, my faith waivered and I just asked for a sign. I prayed,

> "God, my faith is weak, can you please send me a sign- to help my daughter say "Daddy?"

Keep in mind, I did not ask God for me to hear her say "daddy," I just asked Him for her to say it. As parents often do, I closely watched my daughter for any sign of slowing or even regression of the disease. We went to regular doctor visits to check on her condition and get the professional prognosis. At every visit we asked, "How much longer would she live?" The answer sounded worse each visit, while the answer was the same, "We expect her to expire in less than six months." However, God allowed her to stay with us for three more years. You talk about bad weather forecasters. They were wrong for three years. That made us believe they could be wrong for ten more years! Although I did not get healing, I did get more time with her. But time was not enough, so I continued to pray for complete healing into our rag-doll like daughter. As doctor visits came and went with the same dismal results I grew weary and bargained with God,

"Can she just say *daddy* just one time?

I felt things would be better if God showed me a sign. Then I could be sure my daughter's soon to be eternal home of heaven was real, and the Bible's plan for getting there was true. I just wanted the consolation prize I thought I deserved.

But, no luck.

So my faith dwindled as her functions decreased. The disease stole her life one brain cell at a time. She had progressed as a normal baby until age one, hitting all of the milestones parents like to track. Her mother led the charge for her healthcare and was very diligent with every health issue to do whatever was possible. I was consumed with trying to keep things as normal as possible. I did what I could to love and care for her while trying to live in each moment of life we had been given. I nervously left her healing in God's hands if He so chooses. After all, heaven would be a better alternative anyway. Sometimes the wistful dream of heaven was not enough and reality painfully coughed through my faith.

"Breathe Nicole, honey, breathe!"

I would say to her in a coughing episode. In these moments, I allowed myself to feel and the pain as she coughed, seemingly unending. "Maybe she was trying to say Daddy!" I thought, keeping hope alive.

ೋ *PRAYERS ANSWERED IN GODS WAY* ೋ

After she died, our hearts were broken, nevertheless

I leaned on God for answers and healing, knowing she was in a better place. I felt God was all I had left and I was in a habit to pray for my daily stresses, taking care of Nicole.

In my mourning, thoughts of God not giving me a sign – weighed heavy on my heart. I wrote a poem titled "*Daddy she never said.*" In this poem, I compare my girl's agony with the sufferings of Christ. This helped me see my pain in view of the cross and helped my faith. I eventually healed and moved on with a new outlook on life. In time I found myself remarried with a stepdaughter, and a new baby girl. When my new baby started babbling, the first word that was legible was

"Daddy."

For the first two months the only words she said was daddy. It was almost creepy! I had never told anyone about my prayers for Nicole to say daddy. I had forgotten about it until she started talking, "Daddy." When My new baby first said daddy I instantly flashed back to my prayers for Nicole to say "Daddy." Tears welled in my eyes as I understand the sign from God as Genevieve babbled "Dada, Dada," over and over. He blessed me, for keeping what little faith I had, through the storm.

I am not at all trying to tarnish the memory of Nicole - she was amazing and a spotless angel in her short life. Never the less, I felt the sign. This was just one of the signs that prompted me to write this book. When I discussed the "daddy" sign with my parents, my mother said, "That is not true." Then she explained how Nicole said "Daddy" when they were baby sitting. She said she remembered it very clearly because she acted as if she missed us, and she would not stop saying "daddy." I was stunned! Maybe she was crying out for me. For 14 years I thought God never answered my prayer, but He did! It was just like my mom to not remember to tell me this. She always had many things on her mind with our busy family. Not that there is anything I can do about it now, except to validate -

God knows what He is doing even when I don't hear Him… or see His signs.

I told my mom I was a little disappointed that she did not tell me that, but she said it must have slipped her mind. I was so excited and realized God DID answer my prayer even though I did not see it until much latter.

This kind of thing with my mom had happened before so I knew she was not just making it up. In the moment she told me Nicole said daddy my mind flashed back to another time held back some good news. I interviewed for a scholarship at an electronics school just before graduating from Romulus Senior High School. I was hoping to start in the fall after 8 weeks of Army Reserve advanced training in the summer of 1985. If I did not get the scholarship, I was contemplating going full-time Army. I prayed for God's guidance and hoped to win the scholarship. Despite my prayers, I did not hear any news. I got on the bus back home in the fall not knowing my direction. Little did I know the school had sent me a letter a few weeks before I came home. I had won the scholarship to the electronics school, but she did not tell me about it until I got home. Agh! Here I was contemplating if I should join the full time Army to pay for school if I did not get the Scholarship. The scholarship and saying – "Daddy" both happened as they should have. Scenarios like this help put life into perspective.

God's timing happens for a reason.

Faith means trusting God even when we do not see results or do not get things our way. But still, but I wish I could have been there to hear her say Daddy. But that's ok. Somehow just knowing that she did say it and the many other signs of God's presence gives me peace. For now, I can just envision her saying it, but one day I know I will see her saying it for myself in heaven. I like to think that she said "Daddy" to our heavenly father. Even though she was not capable of praying as we know it, God heard every prayer she ever thought of and He is now taking care of her. Have you prayed for something and seen no results? Know that God has answered you, but you may not have seen it, or that God is answering it in a way that He knows in His sovereign will is better in light of eternity.

HEARING GOD IN THE CODE

Jeff Stimpson told me the following story about how we can hear God better: Several men dressed in business suits were waiting in the lobby of an office, waiting to be called back for an interviewed. The job they were applying for was a Morse code interpreter. Another man arrived and went to the reception desk and signed his name on the sign-in list. He asked the receptionist when would he be called for the interview. She told him he would be called back soon, so he sat back in a chair in the lobby with the rest of the men waiting. There was a lot of activity going on in the waiting room. A couple of the men were reviewing their notes on their phones, there was elevator music playing lightly in the background, and there was some noise in the lobby of people arriving to work. After a couple of minutes, the man that just arrived went through the door next to the reception desk to go back for an interview with the manager. When the man entered the manager's office, the manager said to him

"Congratulations the job is yours."

The man was shocked that there was no further interview. So he asked the manager,

"Why don't you need any further interviewing?"

The manager said "we played a message in the background music in Morris code that said:

"The first person to understand this message please come through the door next to the reception desk and come to the manager's office door, the job is yours!"

Excitedly he said, "You were the first one that responded to the message and came through the door, Congratulations! I've been playing that recording for the past two hours and no one else responded."

Then the receptionist came out to the waiting room and told all of the men sitting there the position had been filled and they could go home now. She thanked them for coming in, as each of them had a puzzled look on their faces.

I think we can all learn something from this story. This idea can apply in any environment: If you are paying attention, listening, and watching for the signs of your environment, you can greatly benefit.

God speaks to us in the little things so that He can act in a big way to show himself, but we have to be prepared to hear Him.

I think this story also is more applicable in being prepared for the moment when the moment is prepared for you. I'm sure it takes lots of studying training and effort to be able to interpret Morris code. Especially when there are so many interferences, distractions, and noises crowding out the voice of what we need to hear. This also comes by being fully engaged in the moment. If the man going for the interview was distracted or not fully paying attention, while "waiting," he would have never gotten the job. **That teaches us the importance of waiting well! Wait with a good attitude, engaged, and enjoying the moment.**

Waiting well in your life season of storms is part of Gods blessing to give you peace and is critical to your breakthrough moment.

If the man going for the interview did not have the mindset that waiting was important, he would have not been fully engaged. This is how God wants us to behave when are faced with enduring a storm.

ঌ *READYING FOR THE STORM* ঌ

This past father's day my daughter and wife gave me a great gift every father would enjoy, a hammock! It was portable with a hammock stand. I put it on the back patio when the weather was nice and then made sure take it off the stand and put away at the end of the day after using it. I took care of it because I knew the weather would beat it up and turn it into shreds much sooner and its usefulness would run out sooner.

After possibly the coldest and longest winter in history, finally spring had broken through. The temperatures changed into the 70's with a mild breeze. It was time to breakout the hammock! My family was enjoying the change in weather by just hanging out in the hammock on the patio over the weekend. While leaving for work Monday morning, I noticed I had left my hammock out on the patio. This past weekend I knew the rain was coming and I should have put it away. Instead, I was distracted with many errands, things on my mind, and taking care of my honey do list. I did not think to take care of my hammock. I thought- "I'll get to it before the storm hits after work." I drove home from work in a terrible storm. On the way home, all I thought about was my precious hammock I left out in the rain! I thought about how this applies to many other areas of life:

Storms in life happen to us regardless if we are prepared for them or not.

While a hammock is a small thing in the grand scheme of life, it represents much more.

If I'm not prepared in the little things of life, how can I be prepared for the big things? Are you prepared for the big things in life? Do we take care of the things that are most important to us? Just like me taking care of the hammock: I knew the storm was forecasted, but I procrastinated and made excuses, especially when I knew better.

We all know.......

hard times are coming in our lives, but do we prepare to meet them in Gods power? Or in our own ignorance do we ignore them? Ready or not - here comes the storm.

There will be sickness, there will be death, and there will be unexpected pain. Am I prepared? Am I preparing those around me like my spouse, my children, and myself? In the moments when storms come we need to be prepared in our lives so that we can hear God's voice and make the best decisions. Think of the ramifications of not being prepared in the following phrases:

- Too bad you didn't have any batteries.
- Did anyone bring any extra diapers?
- We ran out of toilet paper
- Too bad, I don't have any ammo
- They say he didn't have any life insurance
- They were not wearing their seatbelt
- I'm not sure if they will be in heaven or not....

As you can see from some of these situations, the consequences of being unprepared can range from very small and insignificant to life changing. Many times, we prepare in our lives to be ready for insignificant situations, but not the things that are eternal and leave a lasting impact to the world around us. We care for some things like:

"Did you bring the chip dip?"

"Who's bringing dessert?"

There are many things in life where we make it a priority to be prepared, but what about the things that matter – our spiritual life and our eternal home?

Everyone should be prepared for as many situations in life as possible including a party. However, what about the things in life that really matter? The big question we should ask:

Am I aware and prepared for my defining moments in my life?

What do I want the world to know me for?

What do I want my loved ones to remember about my life and my legacy?

What do I want my influence to speak for me?

Whatever your answers are to these questions, you have to be prepared in order to come out victorious. Your defining moments determine your influence, hence the power in your life.

ঌ *PLAYING WITH FIRE* ঌ

When you have lost someone you love there is a sense about you at all times, that at any moment, your world could be shaken. Someone you love could be whisked away from a tragedy or sudden turn of events. It always comes on suddenly, even if you are expecting it.

Sometimes our defining moments hit like a crash from nowhere, will you be ready to meet God in the next instant?

I was on the phone talking with my mother about an accident they recently were in. She was explaining to me her injuries and telling me how she needed to take care of herself. She had fractured her sternum and it was in severe pain but she was grateful to be alive and healthy for the most part. My dad sustained no injuries at all, but was very shocked when the crash occurred. Another car hit them head on and they never saw it coming. Part of the reason they never saw it coming was because the other driver had their headlights off. The other car crossed the double yellow line and smashed into the front driver side of their minivan. They spun around a couple times and they ended up in a ditch on the side of the road. The ambulance rushed the other driver to the hospital, but my parents were relatively fine. As my mom described her feelings and events of that night, she said,

"It all happened so sudden, there was no time to stop and pray not even to yell out - 'Jesus, help me!' You are either ready to go to heaven or not ready."

Later at the hospital as my family went to visit her she said " I'm ready to go meet Jesus, no problems with that. Be sure you're ready because whenever it's your time to go you may not have any time to wait to call on Jesus to be saved. If you're not truly dedicated to God and serving him now, what are you waiting for, you're playing with fire!"

SAVING AND BEING SAVED

My stepdaughter Katrina and I had a rocky relationship in her teenage years. From the time she was 15 until 18 years old I did my best at trying to keep the lines of communication open. I loved her with God's love and thought of her as my own daughter as much as I could. She had a rebellious streak in her that would match any teenager I've ever seen. She just would not accept my love and thought I was always judging and preaching at her, (sometimes I was, but I wanted to keep her from harm). All the while, I was trying my best to save her from many painful things that would come her way in life if she did not change her direction. She had her mind made up that me and her mother were no good for her. She needed to get out of the house and find her dreams. As soon as she turned 18 she left home and went to live with her boyfriend. It was an unhealthy relationship and we thought she should stay at home and finish school before she moved out and got serious with a boy. This was much of the same sensible advice any parent would give. She had run away with the same boyfriend a few times while she lived with us and we tried everything we could to help her gain some direction in life.

They bounced around from friend to friend not having a secure place to live and not knowing where their next meal would come from. For two years she was with this particular boyfriend and we were in fear for her safety. Her mother, Lisa and I prayed for her, claiming Gods promises. By God's grace, I was able to keep a relationship with her and she knew I would be there if she needed me. If she wanted to live by our rules she could stay at our home. This kind of tough love was one of the hardest things I ever had to do. One night while I was at Bible study I received a text from Katrina asking me to come get her. You see, she was in a very dangerous, controlling, and abusive relationship. The boyfriend had a violent streak and nobody knew what he would do when she tried to leave.

As it happened, one night while I was at a men's bible study I received a text message from her: *"Help – come get me."* It was Gods perfect timing – that I was at bible study when she texted me. My heart was open to Gods will. I told the pastor to pray for me. I needed to leave immediately and was going to rescue her. I was afraid of what might happen because I had gotten into a few heated arguments with the boyfriend before. He had been violent towards me, but I was able to escape an all out brawl with him. I made the wise choice to call the police to meet me there. I wanted to make sure I could get her safely since she wanted to leave. Little did I know there were other calls to the police station at the same time. Neighbors and a roommate called also because there was loud arguing about Katrina trying to leave that disturbed the neighbors. God gave me strength, wisdom, and courage to be there for my stepdaughter. I brought her home that night with the help of several nice police officers. She was a broken soul that needed healing. After an adjustment period, Katrina was able to stand up on her feet again heal from the broken relationship. She was able to see just as I was there for her, God is there for her always and desperately wants a relationship with her.

Just as much as I was desperate to save her, God is desperate to save us, from our sins, from ourselves, and for an internal destiny with him.

In many ways, I think of Katrina like my spiritual life how God loves me. Katrina did nothing to deserve my love as a stepchild, but I tried my best to love her as though she were my own flesh and blood. I made great attempts to treat her as a true child of mine. Granted I am a very flawed man, but with God changing my heart, I can love her better.

I'll be honest; I did this for some selfish reasons. First, I realize how deep the chasm of my sinfulness is compared to God's righteousness. If it was not for Jesus taking my sins and the penalty of death, I would not be able to be called God's child. I am like a stepchild of God. There was nothing I did or could ever do to become part of God's family. But it was His grace and mercy that reached out to me on the cross. God stretched out his arms and said "I love you this much," as He died on the cross. Whenever Katrina did something horrible: lied to us, hurt us, and the sleepless nights wondering if she was alive: my thoughts would eventually go to the cross. I thought of the wrongs I have committed and sins that God forgave. This gave me the courage and strength in his power to love her and to reconcile her to me, but most importantly to God. I think about how Katrina 's life would have been different if I had not been there for her. I'm glad I was there and prepared spiritually and mentally to have an open heart, open mind and follow where God led me.

Secondly, Katrina is a wonderful person that has a heart full of love and is always looking for a wounded soul to help. Even when, I first saw her in the church row next to her mother, she had a heart to love and restore people. Her mother was tired of not finding Gods man for her, and I had just sworn off women forever if need be. However, Katrina with her bright smile and big brown eyes was sent as a sign to me. It was if God was saying to me:

"Her desire to have a loving father is the same desire I have for God to love me."

God knew I had lost a wife to divorce and daughter to death. In His perfect timing, He put a lost mother and daughter together with a hurting father and son. I instantly told God what a strange sense of humor He has - to give me a stepdaughter the same age as the one I lost and a beautiful Woman that loves God to help me heal. Katrina -She had a missing hole in her life - a daddy; I had a missing hole - a daughter. She has a heart seeking a home and to feel Gods love. Much like most of us, if we would admit it – In her pain she desired to be a restorer of the hurting. The first time the girls visited my son Zac and I, she brought him a squirt gun and me some flowers. Her giving nature lights up the room. Most importantly I'm able to look past her wrongs into the value that Gods sees in her to a dad's life, to a brother's life, and to many other lives. I wanted the girls to complete my family. That is exactly what God knew I needed, to mold my character's rough edges and teach me about His love.

MISSING THE STORM

My new wife and I married on a beach in Jamaica at sunset on a day when a hurricane had just missed the island. I took this as a sign that my life would be filled with near misses from the many storms in life. However,

God will be there in the rain as He is in the pain to put my new life together.

At times in life when we have near misses with storms, we take inventory of our lives direction. We wonder why God allows bad things to happen and why we have near misses. I've had a few near misses in life where me or one of my loved ones could have almost died or had a serious injury of some kind. These "close calls" are a sign from God and a wakeup call.

Many years later my current wife and youngest daughter, Genevieve, went on vacation to the beach and they wanted to swim in the waves. There was a warning sign that said "be careful of the rip tide is very strong today." I knew they had a risky adventurous streak in them and nothing was going to deter them from playing in the waves anyway they wanted to. I was safely tucked onto my towel with a book and a sun umbrella watching them go further and further out into the dangerous waves. I had a sense as I was praying to God that I needed to take action. I slowly walked to where they were swimming because I knew they did not want me complaining and nagging at them to follow the rules. I wanted them to be safe, read the warning signs, and not swim out so deep.

They did not heed the warning signs!

I carefully crept further out into the water trying to avoid an argument. As their playing got further and further out and more dangerous, I moved up my stalking to come closer to them. Praying all the while moving closer, I finally was just within my distance to swim to their aid.

Suddenly, the waves began to mount over their heads. I read the expression on my wife's face as it became pale and full of dread. I knew they were in trouble because I rarely seen her so scared. As the waves took my five foot girls both under water, I dived out to my daughter and grabbed her arm. I tried to pull her to shore and she was screaming at me how much I was hurting her arm. Trying to avoid an argument - I yelled at her "a hurt arm is better than dead, now come!" I continued our trek as my wife was yelling at her to:

"listen to him and go with Daddy!" My daughter allowed the pain and quit fighting me as I helped her to shore.

My wife desperately flung her snorkel out into the ocean, freeing her hands to swim with all her might to save herself. As God's blessings would turn out, we all ended up safely and exhausted on the dry beach.

I think we all learned a valuable lesson that day about the preciousness of life not to mention following the advice of the safety signs. For me it was about following God's signs and listening to his spirit. This was a near miss for each of us to learn what we value most in life and what pleases God. Value each other and obey God! Also, we need to learn when to save others and when we ourselves need to be saved. Many of us do not like the feeling of helplessness but we need to be helpless sometimes in order to heal. My wife did not like me telling her to come in closer to safety, but maybe she should have listened. In the moment of decision, my youngest daughter, Genevieve had a decision to make to,

go with Daddy even in the pain, or keep on fighting against the one who wants to save her from herself.

She had the choice to believe her parents and be saved or not trust and go the other direction and be swept out by the waves. At some point in life we all have to choose to believe God and be saved or go our own way. I'm glad my girls finally obeyed and were saved. But how often do we all really listen to Gods voice to be saved? When God calls us to go with Him, hopefully we will not be enticed by getting too close to danger, but choose to listen to His wisdom.

LOSING MY GIRLS IN THE STORM

I look at my two girls I have now and can't help but think, If I had not lost my first daughter, I would not have either of my two new daughters. The "what ifs" can go on and on. The reality is, I do not know the future, but I know the one who does.

My job is to trust God that He knows what He is doing when my life goes dark.

I could not save Nicole from her terminal illness, but God can.

Even though she died, faith means believing His plan to take her home to heaven and she is waiting for my reunion one day. To have this "blessed outlook" I had to choose to trust Him. I let go of my way of thinking that – It is my responsibility to save those I love. Sometimes I can't save them! I had to let God save them in His way.

The storm of death took Nicole when I could not save her. However, God did! His way of saving her was to take her to heaven.

I did not understand the plan and I did not know why, but by me trusting Him, He released me from bitterness, brokenness, and allowed His spirit to work in my life.

When my stepdaughter ran away, I learned how to forgive and love better. God knew what she needed before she would bend her knee and look to Him. He also taught me how to love and about how deep his love is when we act like a prodigal child. My wife and I could not save her from her own bad choices. Many times, we had no clue where she was and had many sleepless nights worrying. Again, my job is to trust God that He knows what He is doing when my life goes dark. The storm of pride and hard heartedness took Katrina away when I could not save her. God did! His way of saving her was to allow storms to teach her about Gods mercy, grace, and forgiveness. I did not understand the plan and I did not know why but by me trusting Him, He was and still is molding my character to be what we are all called to be - more Christ-like

When I kept faith and accepted Gods will in my storms that eventually allowed me to go with Gods plan. God saved my stepdaughter from an abusive boyfriend and saved my wife and daughter from the riptide. In both these cases they still had to go with me. I didn't do all the saving; I was only following His spirit. By myself it would've been impossible if they fought me when I was trying to save them.

It's not Gods plan for you to be pulled out by the riptide of despair when life's storms hit you. We want God to save us but we have to choose to follow Him no matter the cost.

Even though we don't know what the future holds or what the plan is - that's the essence of faith. When the waves are calling us to come out and play, but then when we get stuck in a storm, we need to learn to hear His voice and - to go with Him.

I knew the story of the prodigal son and always thought God never took action and responsibility for the son's sin and squandering. I always thought God did nothing until the son came back to repent. While that is true to some extent, while Katrina was gone I reread and studied it deeper. I learned that God is always looking and ready for our hearts to turn back to him. He is working out situations that will help bring us back to Him. He is running after you and me even in times when we are rebellious to Him. God had an open heart, welcoming His child to come back home. It is His amazing grace and love that draws us back to our loving father's arms. I never felt Gods love more than when my daughter called me, trapped in sin and captured by Satan's scheme living with abusers. While my daughter was gone, I sought Gods word to give me wisdom. In Luke 15:17-20 God displays His heart toward the prodigal son:

> "When he came to his senses, he said, 'How many of my father's hired servants have food to spare, and here I am starving to death! I will set out and go back to my father and say to him: Father, I have sinned against heaven and against you. I am no longer worthy to be called your son; make me like one of your hired servants. So he got up and went to his father. But while he was still a long way off, his father saw him and was filled with compassion for him; he ran to his son, threw his arms around him and kissed him." (NIV)

Then I remembered the times God forgave me and He ran with open arms to welcome me back after my wandering. I then knew and felt Gods love flowing through me to forgive and love my daughter.

He came running for you and me
– while we were still a long way off.

I knew I would be there when she was ready to come home, not just to my love but also to our Fathers heart!

In her cries for me, I realized God came running after me so I can do the same for others, that is His amazing grace.

Secret 2

Endure the Eye

Chapter 4

Learning to Pray

"Hold on to me Jesus, I'm falling all apart
hold me ever tight . . . calm my restless heart."

BY DEBORAH ANN

⚘ *ENDURE THE EYE* ⚘

In life storms it feels like your very core will fall apart. The worst periods of my life felt like the eye of the storm was hovering over me. I was in the eye during the five years of my daughter's disease followed by a year of searching after her death. Then shortly after that, a period of recovering from my divorce. And finally, just so I can relate to more people's pain, I also had a few years with my runaway rebellious teenage stepdaughter. In these painful storms, I was caught in the eye of the storm. In this section of this book I share my secrets I learned to find blessings in the eye of the storm. Maybe you've been here before. Have you ever been in a situation where it feels like the storm is sitting right on top of you with no way out? This is when you have no power on your own to escape it, but have to look to God to remove the clouds. Secondly, in the Eye of the storm there is a strange peace and calm.

Although everything around us is pain, destruction, and death, God wants to show us a way to *Endure the Eye* of the Storm to come out victorious, give God the glory, and receive His blessings.

Depend on Christ as your hope in these times of trials, because you know that He has a bigger purpose in the Eye than what we can see with our human eyes. In a spiritual mindset, we can see the bigger picture. James 1:2-4 (ISV) views the storms of life this way:

> *"Consider it pure joy, my brothers, when you are involved in various trials, because you know that the testing of your faith produces endurance. But you must let endurance have its full effect, so that you may be mature and complete, lacking nothing."*

Enduring the storms of life takes hope that is not of this world, and depends on trusting in God no matter what the outcome. We all face trials where it seems like the Eye of the storm is hovering over us. When this happens, God asks us to endure because it is part of His plan. When we pass the test we will be mature and lack nothing. It all starts with prayer. I did not learn how to *Endure the Eye* of the storm until I learned how to put everything aside and get serious with God in prayer.

IDENTITY THEFT TO IDENTITY MAKE OVER

I closed the door on my soon-to-be ex-wife and our eight-year-old son. I watched them as they pulled out of the driveway of our small 3-bedroom ranch. I briefly thought of many times she drove out of the driveway going to Bible study, the grocery store, or over a friend's home. The silence of my home snapped me back to reality. Our lives were filled with many years of stress and worry with our terminally ill daughter. We tried everything we could to enjoy a normal life, and now I could. As I grasped for normalcy I realized this was my first weekend alone after the loss of our daughter. In less than three months, I had lost half of my family, both my girls were gone.

Now, it was just me and my boy. As long as my son was in the house, I had to hold it together. I ***could*** hold it together - for him and with God's help. I had to conceal my pain and be strong to make it seem like things were ok for the two of us. I wanted us to be just two normal guys hanging out together leading a normal happy life. The nurses' aides who had been in the house were a comfort when it was just the kids and I. Just having another adult in the home helped. Before my wife left, I felt they were an unnecessary crutch that stymied family togetherness.

I held back the sorrow of losing my little girl and pretended to be strong. Looking back, maybe my ex-wife needed to see me be weak, coming unglued! But I kept myself together, faking all the answers. The downside of having nurses' aides helping care for our daughter was no intimacy in the home. How can you be open and vulnerable always feeling like someone is watching you? With a nurse's aide in our home for 3 years, 24 hours a day, it's hard to show weakness and pain in the face of strangers. Many times I felt, 'Please everybody leave!' And now they had: no nurses, no social workers, no comforting friends offering sympathy, no daughter, and now - no wife and son. Now I could take a good hard look at who I was. Have you ever taken time to be alone for a weekend, a day, even just one night? **Sometimes our storms force us to be alone, truly alone with our thoughts and God.**

Many times, I depended on the white noise in my home to comfort me. I felt my storm was not so bad if I was not alone. Also, I was uncomfortable being alone because I grew up in a loud home. I can relate to when God said it was not good for man to be alone in the book of Genesis. Do you feel the need for some background noise? Like the TV or music?w Now we also have the added noise of social media that competes for our time with God. I have learned sometimes God can only speak when everything else is turned off. He wants you alone and that is enough for Him.

In spite of our feelings, we need to turn down the noise in our lives to hear God. Then He can work on who we really are in light of His word. That is when we can clearly hear direction from God through His word in our subconscious as He answers our fears.

In my darkest storms, I felt as if my Identity was stolen. Like a thief stole my life. Then I am reminded what God says about Satan as the thief in John 10:10:

> "The thief comes only to steal and kill and destroy; I have come that they may have life, and have it to the full." (NIV)

Through prayer and Gods word, I learned to conquer the Storms Identity Theft that brought me to a Christ Centered Make Over. When I saw my life through His word, my storms turned into blessings.

The table below shows how the changes can occur when we see our storms in the right perspective:

Identity Theft Makeover	
Storm Identity Theft	**Christ Centered Make Over**
Storm of loss causes me to lose my identity and roles I play in life.	Secure in my identity and anchored in the veil of Christ's saving grace.
Feel violated and robbed because the storm took my most valuable possessions.	Fulfilled no matter what storm comes because God's promises are my most valuable possessions.
Hard to trust new relationships. Relive old hurts, Blaming others, Excuses for own wrongs, denial of any wrong doing.	Learn to trust again with faith and rely on the love of God to restore my needs, but also owning my problems, taking accountability, and acting responsibly for my restoration.
Victim mentality, complaining because everyone is against you. Hiding wrongs from yourself and others. Believing God is against you.	Live a victorious life because of life in the light of the cross. Uses your storm as a cross to identify with Christ. Blessed life thankful for ALL things believing God is for you.
Jealous of those not in a storm. Self righteous and Proud of self.	Praise God in my storm, knowing He makes all things work to my good.
Cling to bitterness and loss. Loneliness, anger, and resentment.	See my weaknesses as a strength and a gift God will use for my good. Freedom to love myself, joy and authentic life.

In the storm, we have losses that can turn our hearts to Christ and gain His perspective. Gods view teaches us to choose wisdom over foolishness and to choose gain from the pain of storms. Our transformation from storms to blessings starts when we pursue God by learning more about him as in Romans 12:2,

> "Do not conform to the pattern of this world, but be transformed by the renewing of your mind. Then you will be able to test and approve what God's will is--his good, pleasing and perfect will."

When we seek God with our whole hearts and dedicate time and effort to getting to know who he is, God promises to draw near to us and begin our transformation. It is important to speak life into our storms that the enemy wants to use to destroy us. God has given us the weapons to wage spiritual war and win, but we have to pick up the weapons, learn to use them, and realize the real battle is for who think you are, your mindset, and can only be won we we place our hope in *being God's child with every battle.*

We have to remind ourselves ever day, every hour, and sometimes every moment that our Identity is with Christ the Victor over our storms!

ೋ *HEAVEN IS FOR GODS CHILDREN* ೋ

IN MY STORMS my business analyst brain was talking to my heart, trying to solve the puzzle. What to fix? What can I do? What are the next steps? What can I measure? What can I do! After all, there has to be SOMETHING I CAN DO! I struggled with how to be helpless, to be broken, just "being" and not "doing." What do I do when I can't fix it? Is there nothing left to do? It's all been done or tried. No more doctors' visits, no more prayers for Nicole to "Sleep peacefully"; or "Help her, Lord, to breath peacefully tonight," and "Lord, help keep my family together." The time for those prayers was over. Nothing left to do except feel, the thoughts of final conclusion, FAILURE!

It's like spilled milk - it can't be undone: My daughter was already dead! My wife had already left! "What do I do?" I cried out to God.

Looking back now on these darkest of times in my life, I realized I couldn't do anything. My identity was tied up in what I did in my relationships as husband and father. And now, both had just taken a huge blow! I knew to be cautious to not get too wrapped up in my identity at work. I felt I was who God wanted me to BE – a Father and a Husband, that should be my top priority.

Now I was an Ex-husband and a failed father with one less child. I had just lost a huge part of me in the process, a sense of who I am. I had lost me!

On a fateful Friday night, I found myself alone with God in my prayer closet. I had no relationships to DO, nothing left but just to "BE" me.

Without my relationships helping to prop up my identity, I felt like a kite without a string, adrift on the wind. I was a foreigner in the world of the "just being"... Just being a child of God.

In Mathew 19:14 Jesus said I needed to be open to Him like a child.

> "Jesus said, "Let the little children come to me, and do not hinder them, for the kingdom of heaven belongs to such as these." (NIV)

I was not feeling like a child of God on my way to heaven. I was stuck in a performance relationship culture:

Doing for my wife,
Doing for my kids,

Doing for my job.

Now apart from them, who am I? In the Eye of my storm, I eventually learned to put pause on "the doing" and learned to just be. I realized that throughout each of the storms in my life I had a consistent theme:

"I don't know how to just *be*." When pain put my life on pause, I learned to depend on God alone.

I learned to be alive again in the midst of the pain of my personal storm. Only then did I realize He loves me regardless of what I do.

He just wants me to be His child.

Act like His child.

Believe like His child.

And enjoy the life of being a child of the King!

All of my doing led to brokenness and now God was telling me it was ok. "I am enough, when you have run out of you."

ஃ *FROM BROKEN HEARTED TO HEALING* ஃ

When my Ex-wife had our son for the weekend I could truly let it all out, let it all show. I think I was afraid to let weakness show. I wanted my family to depend on me to get them out of the storm. I was being the man; the hero we might call it. At some point after the funeral, I realized we hadn't made it, I had failed. This is one of my blind spots; I'm sometimes too optimistic. Now reality was in the driver's seat of my mind. I wanted to let loose, let my emotions go, and let the tears fall.

The logical optimist was bound up and gagged in the trunk of my mind and emotion was staging a coup.

I was afraid if I let just one tear out, the dam would break, and I would not be able to stop. But now, on this particular Friday, I could let myself go. Then by the time Sunday night rolled around I could let him out of the trunk to run the nine to five shift. As she drove out of our neighborhood for a mother-son weekend, I ran to my bedroom for some Father-son time of my own. For the first time since the prognosis 5 years earlier, I had a heart-to-heart with God. I balled my eyes out into the pillows of my bed. I remember the dogs acting crazy, like I was of the canine variety. I retreated to the closet where they could not bug me. In the stillness of the dark walk-in closet, I felt the silence of my loneliness all around me. **Now in a broken, emotional state, the silence of the closet felt like a warm hug. I buried my face in the carpet as I cried out to God.** At first I tried to pray, but could just uttered strange sounds from a desperate soul. Then thoughts started to form cognition as I prayed short questions. "Why, God, why? Why am I going through this pain?" I realized this secret of God's word in Psalms 34:18

> *"The Lord is close to the brokenhearted and saves those who are crushed in spirit."* (NIV)

I knew He was where my help came from but I could hardly speak. I just knew I could pray and God would help me. I knew the Holy Spirit would intercede for my lack of words. All the years of preparation in the peaceful times brought to mind God's Word. My mind began to answer the questions my soul was asking. I found emotional and spiritual release as I wrestled with God through my pain that night. I felt my healing beginning as His words gave me hope. I poured my heart out to Him in the hours of my darkest night, I felt Him the nearest.

☙ *WRESTLE IN THE CLOSET* ☙

My deepest pain is also the time of my deepest prayers when I would not let God go and He would not let me get away. In the book **Spurgeon on Prayer and Spiritual Warfare** Charles Spurgeon says this about urgent prayer:

"Cherished Personal Experiences: The most important is the memory of what has happened to you...the power of prayer.... Have you ever wrestled with an Angel and come away victorious?"

He goes on to explain the idea that

we need to have moments where we cry out to God in our secret prayer closet and demand He give us something we can have hope in - for a future better than we have at the moment.

That we can also cast our cares on Him and He will help us in our moment of grief to see His face. That was my moment in the closet. That weekend I knew I would be alone. I could have planned to be conveniently busy, or to move on and numb my pain with "others" voices. His Spirit spoke through my conscience to remind me to be wise with my time and what I allow into my mind determines my healing and my future.

The enemy wants to distract me from God time with the cares of the world or an intoxication of any sort. However, I knew what I had been through needed the biggest drug of them all – God.

When I locked the door to my bedroom, went into my closet and hit the floor, I sobbed out my pain and sadness. In the process of venting to Him, I realized the focus of my pain shifted from my circumstances to me personally. I realized I was taking this pain as a personal failure. I could not keep my wife happy, I could not save my daughter from this illness. Something I did was – to blame myself in my prayers. But then I realized – all of my pleas were blaming myself with no relief. My self-pity was telling the lies of the devil that I deserved my pain. Then I realized true deliverance would come from what I knew about God's word:

> I said, *"I am to blame for not being a strong man for my wife."*
> Jesus said, ***"My grace is sufficient for you... my strength is made perfect in your weakness."***
> I said, *"My sin made my daughter die."*
> Jesus said, ***"All who abide in me will remain alive in Christ."***
> I said, *"I should have done more to be a better husband."*
> Jesus said, ***"Unless God builds the house, the laborers labor in vain. – I gave each of you free will."***

And so on, it went for what seemed like the whole night, but it was only for a few hours. As I poured out my heart, blame, guilt, ashamedness, He answered each cry of sin with His love, His word. He caressed each tear with His compassion; He had let His own son die, too. He knew my pain, my loss and my grief. I did not know exactly, but felt He promised me blessings would come from this tragedy.

I just had to keep my faith alive and He would be there for me, giving me hope for tomorrow and each day, one at a time. That was it! It was settled! From then on the answer was the same each day – I will be with you – one day at a time if you feed on my word.

Even while writing this book I'm not sure I can do it. The answer is the same for my daily fears and doubts about the direction of life now. His answer is always the same – His word:

> I say, *"I am not worthy to do this."*
> Jesus says, *"My grace is sufficient for you."*

I say, *"Who am I to speak of your goodness."*
Jesus says, ***"You are a child of the king and heir to heaven."***
I say, *"I'm a failure."*
Jesus says, ***"You can do all things through Christ who strengthens you."***
I say, *"They will mock me and ridicule me."*
Jesus says, ***"They mocked me and ridiculed me. I will use your story for good."***

GOD IS THERE IN YOUR SORROW

MY ANGUISH AS I PRAYED REMINDED ME OF THE STORY OF HANNA IN THE BIBLE. SHE prayed to the Lord weeping bitterly. And she made a vow saying:

> "Lord Almighty if you will only look on your servant's misery and remember me and not forget your servant but give her a son then I will give him to the Lord for all the days of his life and no razor will ever be used on his head." (1 Samuel 1:10 11 NIV)

Hannah prayed to the Lord of hosts in her time of sorrow. She had the right attitude in her time of loss as a servant to God. In that moment, she also committed her whole life to God. That was her wrestling with God moment. She prayed and asked for what she needed, a son. I lost my wife and daughter and I lacked the confidence to pray for what my heart wanted, (the hole in my heart where my girls had been). As I searched for answers in the weeks and months after my daughter's death, the divorce seemed to be eminent. The separation evolved into a normal routine: visitation time, the awkward school meetings, and we each found new circles of friends. We stretched boundaries and moved on in new directions. The desire was strong to get over the crisis and feel good again. Feel good in any way possible, and our roads for healing lead to two different paths.

Realization sunk in - she was not coming back. Our day in divorce court came and went quickly. I could not separate the pain of losing my wife with losing my daughter. The judge was sympathetic to us and granted the divorce in lieu of the 6-month waiting period because of what we had already gone through. For me, it was like watching a car wreck in very slow motion. Now that she was gone, we both just wanted the pain to stop and move on with our lives. I felt we both represented pain to each other. God wants us to live in peace and harmony and that was not where we lived when we were together. I reluctantly accepted the divorce as a means to peace. Now I depended on God to show me the the way to make a new life without a wife. I was brought up that divorce was frowned upon; it was a stigma of something inferior about those who had divorced. I now found myself in that group, a group I once thought of as being leprous. I am unclean! I think this was another lesson God had to show me.

All of us are failed people who need Gods love, grace, and forgiveness every day and that included me.

This legacy of a failed marriage is a constant reminder to not judge others as having failed in their lives because so have I! When I was in my prayer closet, I prayed much like Hannah. I prayed for healing in my loneliness and the loss of my girls. Hanna prayed bravely for what she wanted then acted on it - trying to have a son with her husband.

Many times in my professional life I was called on to fix software or hardware issues. I would find defective parts to repair or replace them. I tested software, ran bug fixes, upgrades, or some other combination to get the system up and running correctly. I was good at that and my default thinking is always:

"**What can I do to fix it.**"

This time there was nothing I could do but give God my brokenness and pain. Learning that I am broken and it is "ok" did wonders for my healing. It also let me off the hook for knowing how to pray or what to pray. I just gave it to Him and tried to live the life God wanted me to live the best I knew how. Did you ever find yourself at a loss for words on how to pray because the pain was too much? That's when we need the Word of God to speak to us, in our lost state when no obstacles are in our way. **I realized by not praying specifically for an outcome, I was ready to listen and could let God truly work in my life.**

He would bring me healing if I let go of control and leave my future up to Him. I learned the freedom of living in the moment because the future looked too painful. I could now let God decide my future.

When I prayed during the stormy days, I did not ask Him to give me something to replace my loss but asked for a sign of His presence for emotional healing. I did pray for those things that hurt. I wanted my son to know I went to God for my comfort and I wanted him to do the same in his pain.

I dared not ask God to give me new girls to replace my old girls, but secretly – I thought it, and God still knew my thoughts! He knew I grieved for them and my heart was broken. I lived with the reality that my daughter was dead and my wife was gone. Sometimes I thought God took them away from me, so I must have deserved it. It is not as if I prayed for God to erase everything that happened because there was nothing left to undue, nothing left to "fix." Slowly, I learned all over again to put my trust in Him.

⚘ *A SPIRITUAL WALK - ANGELS ON THE WAY* ⚘

Putting my trust in God led me to a great spiritual experience with a friend. HE went on a spiritual retreat one weekend. He had been having some difficulties in life - raising three kids, marriage issues, and running a business. I was burdened to pray for him and encourage him to go to this retreat. Part of the weekend plan involved a surprise visit by friends and other believers. They would sing songs of encouragement to symbolize God's angels cheering him on as he sought the Lord's will and clarity. My wife and I had experienced such a weekend and recognized it as a breakthrough in our spiritual lives. They are called *"Walk to Emmaus,"* or *"Via de Cristo."* I sensed a spiritual attack as little things had crept up to keep us from going to the support night. Little irritants began to come between my wife and I. I knew God had blessings waiting and I had to pray through Satan's attacks to be used of God. Saturday night finally arrived. The pastor was driving a van and together with another friend, we were having a nice conversation as we traveled to the event. A little distracted, our pastor turned down a one-way street into oncoming traffic. The two lanes of traffic headed straight at us began swerving to our left to avoid hitting us!

Instantly we were all praying and shouting out different directions to the pastor how to avoid a collision. All of us prayed a form of

> *"Dear Jesus, Help us!"*

My wife said,

> *"Turn around right here in the middle of the road."*

Matt, the other passenger said:

> *"Creep up a little further and see if you can squeeze in a parking lot to turn around."*

I said,

> *"Don't do anything, just stay right where you are on the side of the road and wait for help."*

While we were all panicking and praying, the van remained on one side of the road. Our van blocked one lane while cars whizzed around us, honking as drivers screamed at us. A minute or two later two police cars showed up at the same time, blocking both lanes in front of us, a

Miracle! They were gracious to us and did not give us a ticket. In fact, they stopped traffic for us so we could turn around right in the middle of the road. It may have been coincidence or our prayers, but I believe spiritual wars were being fought as God sent angels to rescue us. We were on a mission only for God's purpose to encourage another brother and Satan did not want that to happen. There was no way out unless somebody came to help us.

God's Angels were trying to come to our aide. They were on their way but came under attack from Satan and we had to keep praying and be diligent and spiritually war ready.

God heard our moment of panic prayers. Have you ever thrown up a "Hail Mary" prayer in a moment of panic? Sometimes I think God does not hear, or my prayers are bouncing off the ceiling. I envision someone standing at a microphone asking, *"Is this thing on? Ah, hello, anybody there?"* However, not this time, because in that moment He came when we called, desperate in our prayers. We were helpless and I gave God the credit for sending those two police cars at the right time to block both lanes. We were in a jam with no way out. Have you ever been in a jam where prayer was the only thing left? I wonder what makes one prayer work and one not? At least, not an answer that I wanted. I have learned there are reasons for prayers being answered that we may not be aware of, but God hears our prayers. When we are in a jam there are some things we *can* do to call on God.

IN A JAM? RING THE DOOR BELL

I recently installed a new screen door on my 100-year-old house when I ran into my broken doorbell. We knew the doorbell worked intermittently but did not have time for such a minor project. We were busy with the essential

parts of the house like: electric, plumbing, flooring, painting, and many other more important projects. I remember hearing the chime just a couple times over the past years. As we were working on the doorframe installing the storm door, we noticed the doorbell wires. They ran through the frame of the doorjamb crack, up to the ceiling, and into the house attic. From there, the wires went to the center room where the doorbell chime box is located. After some quick trouble shooting, I was able to figure out the switch was faulty while the "chime box" in the house worked just fine, (It was fun messing with the dogs, every time we got it working, they went berserk). After some reflection on the parts of the doorbell, I thought this was similar to when we pray to God. The action takes place and the call is sent, but many things can be in the way of the message and a return answer.
Does He hear my prayer ringing in His holy place?
Why doesn't He answer?
Do you ever wonder if your prayers are getting through? Maybe the wires are broken.
Where is God when I need Him the most?

When in Enduring the Eye of a storm, prayer is an essential part that has to be working correctly. There are three basic parts of a doorbell: the switch, the wire, and the chime. Each has to be working in order for the message to get through. In looking back at the storms of my life I can see when my prayers seemed to work better and when they did not seem to work at all. As mentioned earlier, God gave me signs that some prayers worked. It is easy to believe prayer works when you can see the answers displayed in your life. In those times it is easy to give credit to a greater power. Then other times God is silent to my pleas. When has God answered your prayers? Do you have a magic formula? I find it ironic that most of my prayers are like the wire in my **door – jamb**. Prayer works best if I think of it like a **Prayer– J. A. M. B:**

JUMP: The **Jump** is a part that connects or acts as a jump to complete the circuit at the switch. Without the Jump, nothing happens and the sound is not heard. In my old house, my jump was corroded so badly that it did not work at all. I had to remove the switch and touch the wires together to make it work. I thought that sometimes in my life I did not jump to pray when I should, when I knew God was prompting me, or my heart was not right. Sometimes I had a corroded heart that is not able to make a connection.

In order to Jump-start prayer, I need the right attitude in my heart. Am I ready to listen to God? And how quickly do I do what He says: Pray-Act-Do.

Sometimes I only *jumped* when I thought of God like an emergency button. When the wires are rusty I could scrape them and force the connection, but it would not last.

To get the connection to last I need to clean them and hard wire to the button. This is like when I clean my heart from sinful habits and protect my heart from evil.

AGENT: The wire of the prayer doorbell needs a channel to carry the signal. Jesus is our **Agent** in our **Prayer– J. A. M. B.** He intercedes for us, pleads our case to God, and is our righteousness to give us an audience with God in His throne room. We are not able to go directly to God unless we have Jesus as our righteousness acting on our behalf.

Many times, I find it easier to relate in prayer and have a conversation with God from who I know Jesus is: His love, mercy, healing, and forgiveness make Him approachable to *Endure the Eye* of my storms.

MUSIC – in our **Prayer– J. A. M. B.** is the chime of a doorbell.

We should make music to God in praises to Him. Regardless of how I feel. I am showing a sign of my hearts obedience when I praise him.

As long as you are alive, you can find a way to make music to praise Him. He inhabits our praises, (Psalms 22:3) and our lives through our music to Him. Music creates joy in our hearts for the Lord. Nehemiah 8-10 says,

> "The joy of the Lord is your strength."

It makes me think of the song by Casting Crowns, **Praise You in This Storm**:

> "I was sure by now, God, you would have reached down and wiped our tears away, stepped in and saved the day..."

The song goes on to tell us how we need to recognize God and who He is. In His nature, He is the God who gives and takes away, regardless of the outcome of our storm, to recognize this Lordship. We should praise Him in the storm!

BELIEVE – in our **Prayer– J. A. M. B.** After you have done the above all that is left to do is believe God heard your CHIME. Believe God will move on your behalf when you have:

- **Jumped** to pray and act as His spirits prompts you; use Jesus as your
- **Agent** to relate His response to your storm and chime into God's spirit with
- **Music** praising him - the next thing we need to do is to **Believe**

"ONLY BELIEVE."

This is the consistent battle cry throughout the obstacles faced by the characters in my friend William Sirls bestselling novel, **The Reason**." Here are a couple of those situations from his book.

> "Storm clouds gather over a small Michigan town. As thunder shakes the sky, the lights inside St. Thomas Church flicker . . . and then go out......
> All is black until a thick bolt of lightning slices the sky, striking the church's large wooden cross—leaving it ablaze and splintered in two........
> When the storm ends—the search for answers begins.
> James Lindy, the church's blind minister, wonders how his small congregation can repair the cross and keep their faith in the midst of adversity. And he hears the words
> "**Only believe."**
> Macey Lewis, the town's brilliant young oncologist, is drawn to Alex, a young boy who's recently been diagnosed with an aggressive leukemia. She puts her hope in modern medicine—yet is challenged to
> "**Only believe**."
> And Alex's single mom, who has given everything she can to her boy, is pleading with God to know the reason this is happening . . . to save her son. But she only hears silence and wonders how she can possibly
> "**Only believe**."

No matter what life sends your way, the answer will always involve you believing what God says about you and your storm. Believe He is working it for your good even if the lights go out, the doctor says bad news, or you lose everything you see. The cross of Christ still has the answers you need. The next time you find yourself in a JAMB, or you are restoring the doorbell on a 100-year-old house, use a **Prayer– J. A. M. B** to Endure the Eye of your storm with prayer.

"P" SHORTCUT TO P.A.S. THROUGH THE STORM

In **Secret 2 – *Endure the Eye*** remember the shortcut to ***P.A.S.*** through the storm is the three chapters of Prayer, Accountability and Sovereignty. In chapter 4 remember to Pray through to get through. Pray by yourself, be okay with being alone. Be okay with just being *His child* and learn to be broken. In your hurting heart, remember God's broken heart for your sins. Pray and wrestle with God for your blessing in the storm. Know that God is with you and accept His way of using pain to mold you to follow Him. Lastly remember the **Prayer– J. A. M. B**. of the prayer doorbell. **J**ump-start your attitude, **A**gent is Christ, **M**usic is the way you praise Him, and only **B**elieve! There are things you can do to jump start your prayers. Ring the bell and He will answer.

Chapter 5

Learning to be Wise

For God knew his people in advance, and He chose them to become like his Son, so that his Son would be the first-born among many brothers and sisters.

(Romans 8:29)

ঌ 4 1/2' CASKET ঌ

The song by Sanctus Real **I'm Not Alright** expresses our raw feelings when we go through storms. Here are a few lyrics that ring true:

"Can I lose my need to impress? If you want the truth, I need to confess.... I'm not alright, I'm broken inside..., and all I go through, it leads me to you"

Only through the storm of loss can we gain humbleness and a new view of ourselves.

The song goes on to explain how we hide behind our pride when in reality we are broken and hurting inside. When I went through my daughter's death, it was hard to find a friend with whom I could be open and vulnerable about my true feelings. When people ask, "How are you doing?" do they really want to know how you are? Are they really concerned or are they just trying to be politically correct? When people ask questions when you are going through a tragic time, what is there to be said? What do you say? What does anyone say? "My sympathies."

Do you want to just ignore the question or pretend as if they never asked, then say what is expected? Do you just lie and say, "I'm doing fine," or some other small talk and then ask in return "How about you?" If I say I'm doing fine, I really just lied about how I'm doing because I'm a mess! Then I return the favor and ask you a fake question. I really do not want to know how you're doing, Because I am in so much personal agony with my own broken heart. Not many words can help in this wounded state, but listening is the gift you can give that can help, lots!

If I were to be honest and answered the question in truth, it would put everyone in a bad mood. It might sound like this:

"How are you doing?"

"I'm doing horrible. My daughter is terminally ill and she is dying soon. How about you?"

Or how about this response:

"How are you doing?"
"Well I'm kind of busy. Just went to the cemetery and picked out my daughter's funeral plot. It is next to an evergreen near the baby cemetery. "

Here's a nice pick-me-up conversation at the water cooler:

"Well last night was a tough one. My daughter was throwing up and had a fever. She could hardly breathe and we stayed up all night cleaning up vomit and diarrhea, hardly got any sleep. So how was your day?"

Then what makes it worse is if the person wrongly predicts what you were going to say, expecting a politically correct gesture, ignoring what you said, and then answers

"Oh great, thanks, bye-bye."

Are we just too busy in our society to have time to listen to others? Or do we lack the capacity for compassion? Seldom do people have the moral fortitude to hear someone's negativity and trials. It is a rare friend with whom you can share your storms and allows you to be honest and open about how you really feel. Not everyone is emotionally strong enough or available enough to listen and really hear your pain. When selecting friends in life, you are blessed if you have at least one friend whom you can call anytime, night or day, and they will listen to you. Everyone needs that person to cry on his or her shoulder, someone to snap you back into reality when your emotions get the best of you. It is even better when that person can also point you to the One who has the answers you can rely on long after you hang up the phone.

That friend can point you to Christ and remind you of God's promises where true hope, strength, and comfort can be found.

Jesus speaks about how a storm can reveal how we build our spiritual house. He describes in Matthew 7:24-27 about the wise and foolish builders. The foolish builder only listened to God's word while the wise builder listened and put it into action. How is your spiritual building? Is it built like that of the wise man, one that can stand up to the storms of life and remain firm? In my storms, the temptation was to look to others for comfort and sympathy. My temptation was to hang out with people having fun to conceal my ongoing grief that nobody could heal except Gods love. What truly felt good was facing my difficulty in light of Christ's healing. My healing was derailed like Proverbs 14:13:

> "Laughter can conceal a heavy heart, but when the laughter ends, the grief remains."

The ache was never quenched until I learned to pray and not play. I went to others to fill the gaps of my life with fun and good times, but what I really needed was time in prayer.

When I got back from playing or being entertained by others' sympathy, I still had a hollow ache from my loss. Only when I disciplined myself to look to God's Word and prayer did I find comfort. Don't get me wrong, fun has its place, but it should not replace time seeking God.

You learn in going through your storm that fun and silliness has its place, but there is a time when the raw hurting reality of your broken heart needs an honest assessment. Only Gods word can quiet the questions and sooth the aching soul. A friend can remind you of Gods word and hold you accountable to seeking the real answers to help you endure the eye of the storm. Sometimes it takes testing the waters to see if someone is strong enough to handle the truth. When someone asks, "How are you doing?" Then you give him or her just a glimpse of your bad situation. Consider it a test of his or her compassion.

If you say, "I just came back from the funeral home and we purchased a 4 and 1/2-foot casket." Will that friend be there to comfort you or will they only think of themselves and how the pain of your statement makes them feel uncomfortable? Will they politely try to change the subject or squirm out of the conversation and leave you holding your pain?

The truth is when a person has a tragedy in their life or something is horribly going wrong, most people want to stay away from you, as if you had the plague. Many friends slowly fade away from those with illnesses because the cost in time and emotional energy are just too high. Sometimes the reality of your life in a storm is a drag on others warped view of reality. Your pain reminds them of the pain in their life they are hiding from. However, we are called to be like Jesus. While it is difficult at times, Jesus is a friend who sticks closer than a brother. This is the kind of friend you need in the storm. Then remember also, when friends go home you always have Jesus through His Word and prayer. Deuteronomy 31:6 says,

> "Be strong and courageous. Do not be afraid or terrified because of them, for the LORD your God goes with you; He will never leave you nor forsake you."

1st Peter 5:7 says,

> "Cast all your worries on him for He cares for you."

There are many more comforting verses in the Bible that can take your mind off worries and remind you from whom your strength comes.

Good friends are ones who will keep you accountable so to not be stuck in the pit of the pity party.

GOT BUMPERS?

I remember when my children were younger and went to birthday parties at the bowling alley. We had the alley put up gutter guards, a form of plastic tube that sat in the gutter. When the bowling ball veered to the left or right of the lane, it would hit the plastic tube bouncing back into the bowling lane. When you have a birthday party the goal is for everyone is to have a fun time and bumpers insure everyone at least hit some pins. In our spiritual lives we need a form of gutter guards, especially when we are hurting. A good accountability partner can help you from falling into the gutter your life. When I was single again, I was emotionally vulnerable and susceptible to being led into the gutter, doing things that are self-destructive. An accountability friend can remind you of whom you really want to be, help you not act in a way that is not matching your authentic goals in life. This person can help you not act the fool. Just like Mr. T used to say in the hit television show **The A Team**,

> "I pity the fool."

He said this after someone made a bad choice that involved a crime. Mr. T wore a muscle shirt or vest that showed his "guns" and was notable for large gold chains around his neck. He usually said this famous phrase with a scowl on his face that implied he was going to make sure they paid for being foolish! **There are also things you can do in your own life to prevent yourself from acting like a fool.** Nobody wants Mr. T to say to them, "I pity the fool." This meant the consequences are coming!

We all have our foolish moments, especially in adolescence where we make silly choices and get into trouble. Just as a car has bumpers in the front and the back to keep everyone inside safe, our lives need front and rear bumpers, should it run off the intended path. The process of maturity is creating your own **life – bumpers**. We each have a different personality and risk level that contributes to our chances of falling into the gutter. For example, I am too cheap to be a smoker so I would never even start because I would not want to waste my money. Therefore, I would not have these potentially bad health consequences.

The first bumper is a consequence that can prevent me from getting in trouble. The bumper of consequences can keep you in your life's lane. Like the motivation to be wise in Proverbs 9:10,

> "The fear of the Lord is the beginning of wisdom." (NIV)

The consequence of violating God's law makes one fear Him and gives us motivation to do what is right. This bumper leads to the bumper of my condition. When I understand God's holiness and my condition as a helpless sinner, I am motivated to seek God's ways to save me. When it comes to understanding how I stack up to God's standards this Bible verse comes to mind in Isaiah 64:6,

> "We are all infected and impure with sin. When we display our righteous deeds, they are nothing but filthy rags. Like autumn leaves, we wither and fall, and our sins sweep us away like the wind."

Remembering our condition should cause us to humble ourselves and bow to his Lordship.

However, we each may need something unique to keep us weak and bowing in humbleness to God. I do things on purpose to remind myself of my Christian life, to hold me accountable. I am aware of this frailty that manifests the bumper in my condition. Here are a couple examples from my life.

For years I drove around in a 15-year-old Oldsmobile because I felt God spoke to me about my pride and how I might be tempted to judge someone by the kind of car they drove.

I have a little bit of an anger issue sometimes while driving in hectic traffic. I put a bumper sticker on the front of my car that says "Jesus Heartbeat of America." This bumper sticker reminded me of my condition that I need a Savior. If I acted like a fool in traffic, others would see me as a hypocrite.

Don't get me wrong, I've had new cars before and I don't always have to have a bumper sticker that says I belong to Jesus to make me behave. However, it is doing the things God's Spirit tells me to do that keeps me remembering my condition. It is a personal conviction for each of us. Do you have a practice that keeps you in touch with your fallen condition? Practicing some kind of remembrance helps keep you accountable to the bumper of your condition. This is not something that is begrudgingly practiced, but honorably sacrificed out of reverence and fear.

That leads to the second bumper - consequences. God sometimes gives these bumpers to us. Paul has bumpers to remind him of his condition as found in 2nd Corinthians 12:5 -10:

> "That experience is worth boasting about, but I'm not going to do it. I will boast only about my weaknesses. If I wanted to boast, I would be no fool in doing so, because I would be telling the truth. But I won't do it, because I don't want anyone to give me credit beyond what they can see in my life or hear in my message, even though I have received such wonderful revelations from God. So to keep me from becoming proud, I was given a thorn in my flesh, a messenger from Satan to torment me and keep me from becoming proud. Three different times I begged the Lord to take it away. Each time He said, '***My grace is all you need. My power works best in weakness***.' So now I am glad to boast about my weaknesses, so that the power of Christ can work through me. That's why I take pleasure in my weaknesses, and in the insults, hardships, persecutions, and troubles that I suffer for Christ. ***For when I am weak, then I am strong***."

There are many lessons to be learned from Paul in this section. Remembering our condition keeps us accountable and to realize our weaknesses. Then we can let God use it as a strength when we surrender our will to his Lordship. Even with bumpers in life, we can still make wrong choices and God allows us to experience some of the consequences that will teach us to be wise and eventually bring us back to a path to serve Him. If a car has two bumpers, so should our lives to keep us going in the path God wants - consequences and condition.

ঌ ***BAD WOMAN*** ঌ

After my divorce was final, my self-esteem was low and I was looking for something, someone, to validate my worth. I wanted someone to say I was still valuable, attractive, and worth being loved. Looking back on it now, I can see I was living according to my emotions rather than what I knew God's Word said of my value. It was as if I was in a country song,

> "Looking for love in all the wrong places."

I thought of women I had dated or wanted to date before I was married. Now that my wife left me, all bets were off, I could do my own thing now, so I thought. Memories have a way of making the past overly romantic and more attractive than it actually was. Looking back on her now, I saw her like the song **Bad Woman** from the song by Kool and the Gang:

> "Every time that I see lovers look into each other's eyes
> I realize the best of my life was you..."

I ended up in a dating relationship with this old flame. I thought she was what I needed and was tired of God's plan for my life, it was too painful. I was now single and not attending the same church that brought me through my storms of disease and death. Their were to many painful memories brought up as I tried to create a new identity as a single man now. This left me alone and unaccountable without familiar spiritual brothers and sisters in Christ in my life. I removed a bumper of consequence. This allowed temptation and a compromising lifestyle to take root. I found myself in a battle with my thoughts.

The wisdom from scripture and my mom's words came echoing in my subconscious:

- Don't date anyone you wouldn't want to marry.
- No temptation is too much for me... God will provide a way out.
- Flee from sexual immorality....

Was I playing with fire... I was doing the opposite of fleeing. I knew too much of what God expected to let my flesh and feelings make my decisions. But slowly they did, when I ignored the spirits voice. While I still had somewhat of a spiritual life, I felt that God had let me down. Part of me felt:

"I'll try my way God, now that I see what your way did for me."

I knew who I was and who God was, but there was not much of a connection because I felt I had no mission in life. My neat, tidy little family had splintered and my mission to raise a godly family had self-destructed. I did still have a wonderful son to live for and to be the focus my attention. My son was easy to please and low maintenance. That allowed me to start dating occasionally.

My first mistake was dating a woman for outer beauty alone and not considering a match for my soul. She had everything I thought I needed. Okay, honestly, she was really beautiful and she liked me and my sense of humor. I can be a very funny person in the right setting. I did not consider if she was a fit spiritually. She had drifted away from any regular form of faith but initially I overlooked it. After a few dates, I started to sober up and realized I did not want to make the same mistakes I did ten years' prior with my now ex-wife. You see, we were not spiritually matched either. For the three weeks we dated I had a spiritual war going on inside of my soul. She had many good qualities to offer, but the cost would be high regarding my core beliefs. I tried to compromise by telling myself I can take her to church; I can lead her to Christ. While I was in an emotional state of weakness it was hard for me to be strong and to show her the kind of man I wanted to be. I made too many compromises to fit in with her environment as I tried to impress her. It is like somebody coming out of ICU who is not ready for a marathon.

Now was the time my *preparing in peace* kicked in. Many of the Bible verses and things I knew about consequences and my condition started returning to my mind as I spent time with my "Bad Woman." I could tell it was not working - she was leading me away from my faith and I was not bringing her closer to mine. I was not ready to show someone the path to Christ when I, myself, was in critical care with my faith. I had some long, drawn-out discussions with my accountability partner and best friend, Larry. He told me in specific words I needed to "dump that girl." We both prayed for her, hoping she would find salvation but at the same time Larry prayed I would come to recognize that this girl was not a good influence on me in my vulnerable condition. After a few open discussions with Larry, he made a bold move to put me in checkmate. He asked me to meet him at church with a pastor and another friend. Together they would pray with me to get rid of this girl. He affirmed what I was feeling, helping me understand she was a bad influence on me. I made the appointment with him and showed up at the church.

As I sat in my car before I went into our secret prayer meeting, I thought to myself, "I'm really stuck in this relationship, but. I like the way she makes me feel about myself," and I had not felt that way in a long time.

I knew I needed get un-stuck and God had something better for me but I had to have faith to believe God was still on my side.

I had to believe He would bless me in ways that would not cause harm to my son. As I was walking into the church, I knew what I needed to do. I would have to walk away from this woman, actually- flee, run! My friends prayed for me and I agreed I would cut it off with her that night. I followed through with my commitments to break it off. I knew I had some growing up to do to find God's plan for a partner.

ঌ *GOOD GIRL* ঌ

While finding my footing in faith I still wanted to find the new Mrs. Right. I felt that person would help me with the next chapter of my life. I also felt the need to have a mother figure in the home for my son. I slowly started finding my confidence as I focused on being the best dad I could be for my son. I thought I needed to change churches because I had too many bad memories of my daughter and now ex-wife at the old church. So I went church hunting. It was a rough phase for me as I really enjoyed the wonderful church from my old life that our family shared. I have only great memories of the church with my ex-wife. However, in order to move forward and be emotionally healthy I needed to live in my new single parent reality and leave the past behind.

I kept on with the dating scene. I started a dating relationship with a good girl. I thought she was the perfect package...but she was not a Christian. (You think I'd have learned!) In any case, she was a really good person and I thought that was a good start. I thought, "maybe I can influence her to become a Christian." We'd been dating about a year when I felt the urge to move in one direction or the other but our spiritual togetherness was not happening. She was leading me further away from Christ. But, she had so many things going for her – good career, funny, did everything ask of her and my family loved her. Still something wasn't right...we were not spiritually yoked. As we got more and more serious my spiritual relationship with God began to drift because of my quagmire with this "good girl".

Once again my accountability partner, Larry, asked me many questions. He wanted to know if this was the right girl for me. I knew what he would ask and I prepared the answers in my mind for when he would ask me. My response was, *"Yes, Larry, I know she's not a Christian but she's a good, good, person."*

I tried to compromise and win him over. Many times I thought I must be exhausting to him; however, Larry and his wife, Jeanne, showed me that love is long suffering.

As I prayed for God's guidance, I once again felt stuck in a performance faith "of doing things" – versus BEING a child of God's.

In spite of my sense of blame, the years of God preparing me reminded me of His wisdom. I thought of direction and encouragement from Gods word:

> *"Go back to my first love - Christ"*
> *"Seek first the Kingdom of God ... and all these things will be added to you"*
> *"He knows you have needs..."*
> *"If He cares for the Sparrow... how much more valuable you are than the birds!"*
> *"If my people will humble themselves... turn from wicked ways... seek my face..."*

I needed to get right with God and do the things I knew to do. As I fell back in love with God, He gave me the strength to follow Him better.

I had been in a wrong relationship before, and now this time I knew what to do. I was emotionally healthy enough to stand on my own spiritual legs. As God's Word gave me strength, I decided to break it off with my "Good Girl." This time I did not needing Larry to tell me what to do, but I coveted his prayers. He supported me and praised God for my difficult choice and that I was finally following God. I regret that I broke this woman's heart. In any case, I had to follow Gods leading. I hope one day she does come to a relationship with Christ and find Gods perfect man for her. After we broke up, I would never see her again. I have learned sometimes God uses different people to reach those I can't reach. I learned I need to maintain a vigilant prayer life to keep from sin and hurting others.

THIS ONE IS JUST RIGHT

After two semi-serious relationships, I decided to give up chasing women. I told God I would only date a woman if He brought her into my life. It had to be Him. I was finished trying to control my destiny in this area. I finally felt free of this burden of needing someone to complete me. **I realized no one else could truly make me happy because I was not living the life God called me to live. I was not happy with who I was, so nobody would be right until I got right with God.** This is my authentic self and core belief to live that I know God wants for me.

Once I realized the authentic self that God wanted me to be, I realized how far I had drifted away.

I discovered that I was seeking the satisfaction, the plans, desires, and the life that other people expected for me. I dated the bad woman who made me feel good but everyone else thought was too wild for me. Then I dated a good girl whom everyone liked, but I felt was wrong for me. In both cases I was not following God, nor did I have a close daily spiritual walk with God. As I became romantically frustrated I sought God and He gave me this word from Psalm 127:1,

> "A Song of Ascents. Of Solomon. Unless the LORD builds the house, those who build it labor in vain. Unless the LORD watches over the city, the watchman stays awake in vain."

That is exactly what I was doing, laboring in vain. Soon after I broke it off with the "good girl," I gave up on women. I told God, "I will not have a woman in my life if that is Your plan." I committed to Him if it meant living as a single man forever that would be fine with me. My plan was now to simply follow God to be the man I wanted to be and to be a good father for by son.

Finally, I felt I learned to be wise in the eyes of God. It was simple and maybe that was the hardest part– to get out of Gods way and leave my unknown future in His hands while I worked on just being His child again.

Soon after my break up with the good girl I was attending a new church and God changed my plans again. I was happily praising God minding my own business in the church pew. As we sang songs I was thankful for my new direction, clarity, and commitment to putting God first. All of a sudden, a little girl and her mother sat next to me in my pew. I noticed the lady was pretty and the little girl was close to the age of my now deceased daughter. I also noticed no wedding ring or man in the area next to them. The little girl gave me smiling glances with a gleam in her eye. As I was praising God for my future in His hands I though

> *"Could my future have just now sat next to me?"*

I prayed to God while singing,

> "God – that would be a funny joke – you know I just said I was done with women and YOU are enough for me!"

I sang a few more praise songs and then spoke to God again.

> "God you know that girl is about the same age as the baby I lost – you know I don't deserve a little girl in my life, not after the mess I made out of my family."

During the remainder of the church service, I had the most remarkable conversation with God. He said,

> "Yes you made some mistakes, but this is all in my plan. Your mission will be these girls. They will not be something you deserve, but someone for you to serve."

From that day forward, we have been together. It all happened organically when I started to follow God, in His timing. It was as though He'd planned things to happen this way. He knew a father and son would meet a daughter and mother at the right time, at the exact moment when we would come together for each other and His plan to bless us both.

Looking back on it now, it reminds me of the fairy tale **Goldilocks and the Three Bears.** The first porridge was too hot, the second porridge was too cold and then the third porridge was just right. Then Goldie locks ate the whole bowl of porridge. It was only when I turned to God that my life tasted just right. Then I could eat it all up! The first time the porridge was hot was very painful and life was not digestible. Then there were times in life when I chose to eat the cold bowl of food. My life was not in harmony with who God created me to be.

Only when I gave up control, God made my life "just right." Many times, I've learned when I do life God's way, He has a plan that is just right for me.

⁂ *ACCOUNTABILITY PREVENTS A PITIFUL FOOL* ⁂

Why did I have to go through all the pain of bad choices in order to find the thing that was 'just right" for me? I realize more and more that my biggest problem is me! My pride, my honesty, being true to myself, learning to stand up for what I believe, not just taking what life hands out, but moving life to the direction I feel God has called me. Through the storms I learned to love and appreciate being accountable - to God's Word, a close friend, spouse, coworkers, and bosses at work. In the accountability, God brings stability. I find rest and peace when I do what I can but then give the rest of worries to God. This is where the healing comes from – when I understand and apply this gift and godly principle. From Psalm 23:2,

"He makes me lie down in green pastures… He restores my soul."

This restoration starts with acknowledging Him, then being accountable, focusing on the right actions in my life. I learned to fight for my healing. I knew I was at risk for doing something stupid, so I found ways to be accountable to a close friend. I took a divorce care program to deal with my feelings. I still made some mistakes, but with bumpers in place, I made it back to a healing path. With the storm clouds rolling past, I had to learn to rest in Him.

With so much of our lives our spent achieving, planning, preparing, thinking, talking, wishing, and hoping all about the FUTURE. In my storms I learned to live in the NOW. I found rest in the *Eye of the Storm.*

The psalmist David speaks about it best. "He makes me lie down beside the still waters…" I believe there are seasons in our life when God has to make us rest to discover His purposes and our peace.

ঌ *"A" SHORTCUT TO P.A.S. THROUGH THE STORM* ঌ

In Chapter 4, we learned shortcut "P" is for *prayer* to P.A.S. through the Eye of the storm. "**Pray through to Get Through."**

Shortcut "A" in P.A.S. is for Accountable: "Accountability to find stability."

There have been many times I wished I had someone to whom I could be accountable but I did not invest the effort to have that fail safe in my life. In the business analyst world, we call that area "controls." Controls limit the loss of process or actions in a particular business area. **Implementing accountability into our personal life can help us avoid a total life meltdown. Accountability can mitigate the implications and unintended consequences of a storm.** In the aftermath of the storm, I lacked accountability and direction and was easily sucked into a pity party. Many people with similar conditions would feel sad about their loss yet not understand or believe their child is now in heaven, healthy, whole, and healed running around in heaven's playground. I could not stay too long without going crazy in this misery community.

Did I just get finished seeing a bad movie or was I really the star actor in the movie of my life? As for my feelings, I was reminded of basic training in the army. Even though it was uniquely painful, we were in it together. While each solider had to overcome obstacles and challenges, we held in common the reality of the shared experience. Now here I was alone with my pain. How do I go on living when everything is changed?

How do I go on having faith in God when He let all of the bad stuff happen to me? I know it sounds weird but after something goes on so long, one can become emotionally dizzy and unsure of God's plans. Gun-shy, er, um I mean *God-shy*.

I sometimes felt:

"if I can just keep God the target of my life – that would be enough to appease Him."

The risk is to make foolish choices while in this frame of mind. Having someone to hold you accountable can limit the number of times one acts like a fool while providing wise counsel. As I learned to avoid foolish impulses, I began to seek accountability and realized its value in my life. It helped me to make better choices and prevented me from making foolish ones.

Just knowing I had to voluntarily report my life choices to someone else kept me from wrecking my life further in the aftermath of the storm. The principal at its root is the wisdom of God's words, from Proverbs 27:17,

"As iron sharpens iron, so a friend sharpens a friend."(*NLT*)

Being accountable means having open and honest dialogue to help us correct our course when storm winds seem to be pulling us in all directions. You need a friend to tell you the truth even if it hurts. Of course, it goes both ways - help hold them accountable for personal goals and controls in their life as well. I heard this saying -

"Problems don't age well."

The shortcut to your life's problems is to accept responsibility for something that might seem wrong. This requires transparency and being comfortable with taking the blame. Accepting corrections and being transparent about it actually shows wisdom. I have learned through my storms how to identify a problem, shed light on the issue, make reconciliation and course-correct as soon as possible.

Many times, I've owed a huge debt of gratitude to a friend or accountability partner for guiding me back to the path of being the man I want to be. This philosophy is also found in Proverbs 27:6,

> "Faithful are the wounds of a friend, but deceitful are the kisses of an enemy."

Many times, I know I am making the right decision, even when it hurts my feelings and it's uncomfortable. In the nursing profession, my wife calls this –

acute pain to conquer chronic pain.

There will be pain in life but sometimes you can choose the pain that makes you better over waiting for pain that makes you worse to come to you. Or in other words:

The pains we choose combats the pains we do not chose.

When we chose pain that disciplines our life back on track toward our authentic beliefs, the rewards may not be seen immediately, but God will honor our turning back to Him in some way that blesses us.

In contrast, when we make bad choices by choosing something enjoyable now while not worrying about the consequences, the future consequences usually produces worse pain. Pain from consequences are usually something we do not get to choose. By adhering to some form of discipline before breaking our own moral beliefs, we avoid pains in our life that are out of our control, regrets.

Pains we chose now are the seeds of blessings and can protect us from future mistakes.

Understanding this principle while in the Eye of the storm can help guide you out of the stormy gales and safely into harbor. I know in my storms it felt like my moral compass was broken, when the people and rituals I depended on for stability was suddenly taken from me.

Only when I learned to not live by my feelings alone but on God's promises did I start to see my way out of the fog.

Chapter 6

Learning to Endure

"And now the three remain, faith, hope and love,
but the greatest of these is love"

(1 Corinthians 13:13)

❧ *HOPE - OUT OF THIS WORLD* ❧

In the movie **Star Trek: Into the Darkness**, after Kirk's heroic actions saved the entire crew, he faced certain death. As his life was fading away he had a conversation with his close friend Spock.

Kirk said to Spock:

> *"I'm scared Spock... help me not be. How do you choose not to feel?"*

Tears ran down both of the men's faces, as Spock uttered in a logical tone:

> *"I do not know. Right now, I'm feeling."*

Throughout the movie Spock, being half-human and half alien, is capable of turning on or off the human feeling part of himself. However, faced with the inevitable death of his best friend, he had no choice but to feel fear.

Part of having someone close in your life is the pain of losing that person. With God in the picture, our humanness has hope in the face of death.

Being human means fully embracing our emotions and one of those emotions is hopelessness. Is fear of death the ultimate hopelessness? Hence, the essence of humanity is facing our hopeless condition.

I once heard survival of all mammals could be summed into our basic needs of food, water, and air. We can survive three weeks without food, three days without water and three minutes without air. Being human adds a fourth basic survival need - hope. We can only survive three seconds without hope.

WHERE IS YOUR HOPE?

When facing a storm many look to the thing they value most to help them through a tragic event. If you hope in money, then you are tempted to think money can save you from life's pain and problems. If you hope in your abilities and your physical natural gifts you may think you can avoid storms by your performance. In either case nothing we have man-made or of our own doing can overcome the storm of death. In that moment when the last grain of sand hits the bottom of the hourglass, we all have to depend on someone or something outside of ourselves.

God tells us life is a contest: a fight and a race. In the battle for faith there are winners and there are losers with the prize of an eternal home with Jesus in heaven.

What is the definition of truly winning in life? I would suggest to you; it is keeping the only thing you can take with you to the afterlife - your faith.

Winners keep their faith strong despite the many storms faced in a lifetime.

This means our faith in Jesus Christ as Savior gives us confidence and the ability to conquer fear, death, and hell. 2nd Timothy 4:7 puts it like this:

> "I have fought the good fight. I have completed the race. I have kept the faith."

I always thought being a Christian was about just being kind and easy-going, but not in the mind of our convictions. Also in Jude 1:2 says

> "Dear friends, although I was very eager to write to you about the salvation we share, I felt compelled to write and urge you to contend for the faith that was once for all entrusted to God's holy people. (NIV)

With the whole family depending on your hope in Christ, you will see storms in a different light. **This is your battle for hope!** When our natural feelings tell us God is not real because we do not see him in our storms and believing in Jesus is for fools, take heart! You are right where you should be.

Life's storms can make you turn to Christ even more and hold tighter to the one thing nobody can take from you: your relationship with Jesus. In the end, that is all that will matter.

ঌ *LOVE IS THE GIFT OF HEAVEN* ঌ

I have bittersweet feelings when I think of the date March 11 every year. **On this day my first daughter went up to heaven while my second daughter came down to earth. How many people can say that?** On 3/11 at 4:05 a.m. my first daughter (Nicole) died. On 3/11 a few years later at 4:35 a.m. my second daughter (Genevieve) was born. In between, I was blessed with a stepdaughter (Katrina). With my first daughter's passing I learned to accept her fate in the hope of heaven.

The closer to death she was, the closer to heaven I felt – because of this hope!

During my emotional healing shortly after her death I wrote a poem that explains this **paradox of hope:**

ꕤ *LOVE NEVER FELT* ꕤ

There you were in the garden, "Take this cup," you cried.
Here am I, in my night that will not end.
My prayers sent up on fallen wings as I fade again.
Why? I cry, as I know the answer is sins cursed her to death.
Her limbs so weak and life so faltering.
Her love flows out through her twisted body.
With torment so great, there must be a
reflection of great joy to be found.
Angels come to visit but nobody is home.
Love never felt and wings never flown.
How? I cry, as I know the answer is love inside.
The hope never fades; the tears never end as I stare at the sky.
"Come home to life from above." He says as she is held down.
Can there really be hope?
is life so profound as
to give beauty to death?
Praise God for the hope of Jesus. Come Lord and
heal my broken lamb.
She has no chance to sin, though her body stained with Adam.
Lost ambitions found in the hope of death.
But, alas, death is conquered in the glory of the cross.
Her breath slows and eyes glows dim as
death beckons again and again.
Can this be the end of another test of the weight of humanity?
Our broken shells are crushed in the sand.
"Mommy hold me," "daddy kiss me,"
she never said, but her love was felt.

We had daily prayers and discussions about her heavenly home. I remember hope feeling so real. I understood in my poem hope in the things of life we can do or see but rather faith in the unseen:

The hope never fades; *the tears never end as I stare at the sky.*
"Come home to life from above." He says as she is held down.
Can there really be hope?
is life so profound as to give beauty to death?

Praise God for the hope of Jesus. Come Lord and heal my broken lamb.

You see, many days we did not know if it would be her last. Every smile was precious. I miss those days of living in the moment of hope and now I think of the reality she is living out in heaven.

What would she say now looking down from heaven? What would my daughter say to her family if she could speak to us now from heaven? What would be her story? I wonder what she would say about my life. Would she be proud of me? Is she mad at God, her parents? Would she be sad for the life she never lived? Would she forgive us for not holding the family together? Would she be cheering us on and be happy with how things have turned out so far? What would she look like as an adult? All of these questions and many more I ponder from time to time when I think about her and my hope.

I see her and my hope in my girls now and it reminds me to live in the hope of heaven.

Even when death does not feel as prominent as it did in those days, my experience helps me remember our hope is bigger than what we see.

It's weird thinking about my family then and my new family now. I just wonder what she is like now. Eric Clapton captures many of those thoughts beautifully in the song **Tears in Heaven**.

> "Would you know my name, if I saw you in heaven? Would you hold my hand...Would you help me stand?

The song goes on, questioning, "...If I will be there in heaven...." and many other questions about the afterlife and our humanity. Toward the end of the song he says that he knows he doesn't belong in heaven, but maybe his daughter can help him get there. Keeping one's faith while in the storm of death is difficult and causes one to wonder "what-if's" and have doubts about faith.

We need to *Endure the Eye* of the storm with faith in the hope of heaven, above the storm! When we change our view to a higher altitude this process changes our attitude. We need to force our mind to focus on Gods higher ways to lift our spirits when we are feeling down. Then God can use our lives for His glory and our good.

FAITH IN HIS SOVEREIGN COMMAND

"Alright you knuckleheads - get into the gas chamber and I don't want any crying." I remember my basic training drill sergeant yelling at me, as a new soldier in Fort Knox, Kentucky. They were trying to break us and we were all fearful of what we might expect in the dreaded gas chamber. It was a room full of teargas and we had to go into this building without our masks on. When we had enough of the pain only the sergeant would tell us when to put the masks on. They made us go through this pain for a bigger reason than just to torture us. As a soldier in that moment, we just wanted to survive, to get through it. They wanted us to experience what the tear gas did to our bodies - the pain in our lungs, the labored breathing, and the swelling of the eyes. The big picture was to teach us what to expect if we ran into this in a combat situation. We also learned to trust the commands of our superior officers, even if it involved pain. We were just to obey and put our full trust, our very lives, in our sergeant's hands. Even if we felt like we could not take it anymore and we had to obey. **Believing in Christ means this kind of trust as a soldier of the cross.**

What if we can't hold on any more and the pain in life is too much to bear? We need to cling to His promises even more when it gets tough. As long as you have breath you can call out to God for hope and a way out. 1 Cor 10:13 says,

> *"No temptation has overtaken you except what is common to mankind. And God is faithful; he will not let you be tempted beyond what you can bear. But when you are tempted, he will also provide a way out so that you can endure it."*

This means He will provide a way out when it seems impossible. He can work for you when it is the most difficult. This stretches your faith to lean on God to rescue you. Keep looking for Gods way out! When it seems impossible – rejoice in the truth and be confident in your faith.

A beautiful picture of God being there when you cannot hold on anymore is from Lindsay McCaul. Her song **Hold on to Me** speaks to the heart of our hope being in Christ:

> *"When I'm not good at holding on to you, you hold onto me."*
> *"I know I need you now....to do what I can't somehow."*

When the storms of life are howling outside, banging on the door and the ground underneath your feet is shaking, we need a hope to hold onto.

I cry out to God to save me and recognized His sovereignty in the very same storms that threatens me.

It is as if I do not believe in God until the moment a giant lightning bolt strikes near me and I instantly recant. We then say, "

God I believe in you - save me."

Our faith can be so shallow and frail at times. That is exactly why God created our faith for us to put our trust in Him. He becomes faith for us. He is the one that starts our faith and He is the one Who finishes our faith.

We can see this from Gods word.

> "Looking unto Jesus the author and finisher of our faith; who for the joy that was set before him endured the cross, despising the shame, and is set down at the right hand of the throne of God." Hebrews 12:2 (KJV)

In that moment when the storm hits and we don't understand why or what good can come of it, we have a choice to make: choose to see we are blessed and recognize God's sovereignty or choose our own stubbornness and pride.

We call out to God in faith in the storm: just like the disciples did in the storm on the boat; like Peter did as he was walking on the water and began to sink; like Jonah did in the belly of the whale; and like Jacob did as he wrestled with God in the desert. Just as Jacob fought for his blessing and many others in the Bible called out to be saved, you and I can fight with God to save us and bless us.

One of God's names is Hosanna, which means "Save Now." Many times, we want God to save us from our pain that this fallen world hands us but that may not be God's agenda. Part of dealing wisely with the pain God allows us to have is to realize His perspective on it. I know my perspective - regardless of God my flesh cries out "I just don't want it for any reason!" Despite my feelings, if I stop and take a step back to consider His purpose for pain, I might be able to deal with it a little better. When I was a child, I would do something wrong and my dad would give me a spanking. Even then I did not want or understand it, but it made me behave as a better child or taught me a valuable lesson. It was not until I was an adult with kids of my own that I sincerely learned to appreciate my childhood discipline my my father.

By God allowing these "spankings" by the world to enter our lives, He is bringing about His plan of restoration. It takes faith to believe that the trials happening to us are really for our good and will eventually lead to our redemption.

It is only natural to want God to intervene and save us from the bad stuff in life, but we should always remember God uses these things to mold us, shape our character, and make us the person He needs us to be. Just like the lesson as a soldier when I learned in the gas chamber. God has a plan for our good and to make us stronger. He is conforming us to the image of Christ.

ঌ *YOUR CROSS - IS YOUR CURRICULUM* ঌ

Our storms are our cross God plans for our lives. God wants to teach us to trust Him in the classroom of our cross. Many times **God's plans are very detailed and describe specifically what to do and how to live.** He also gives instructions on how to survive death and the storms of life. To survive the flood, God gave specific instructions to Noah. To survive Sodom and Gomorra's destruction, Lot's family had to obey the angel's command and *"...not look back or you will turn to stone!"*

There are many more examples where God gives us the lesson plan to survive storms. Hint – There will be a test on His plan for your life!

In the book of Numbers, the Bible describes with meticulous detail what the various tribes of Levites were to do as they moved their camp from place to place. He did this so that they would not die. If someone from the worker tribes touched one of the sacred objects, they would die in an instant. Why is God so harsh? What was the purpose in God killing them? It seems so unloving and extremely harsh. God's holiness is represented here.

How powerful and deadly is His holiness and righteousness! This also paints a picture of how sinful mankind is and how we are incapable of meeting God's pure and holy standards. This symbolizes the huge gap that remains between mankind's holiness and God's holiness. God demonstrates this through the special care the tabernacle workers were to use when setting up the tabernacle instruments. Every part of our heart, mind, body, and soul should be under God's command and control.

In the Eye of the storm, you have to be extra careful that you know the direction in which you are going to get out of the storm. Just like escaping from an airplane that is on fire, you have to follow the directions exactly to get out of the door correctly, even if you can't see. You may have to feel your way around in the smoke to find your way out of trouble. It is very critical in emergencies that one pays special attention to every detail or there could be devastating consequences. It is just like in any other emergency. In the storm, it is more important than ever to be under the direction of the Holy Spirit, read God's Word daily, and take actions to support your faith. Only by following God specific directions will you come out of the eye of the storm with your faith intact and blessings ahead.

In order for Christians to have His mercy, Jesus laid down His life to show us true love and set us free. That is the model set for us, our cross for His blessing. Christ has a high standard and that is why He allows pain to stretch us to grow. Jesus was betrayed, beaten, and willingly sacrificed His life. It is no small thing to understand the reason and meaning of pain in our lives. Ultimately, God wants us to know Him and understand His meaning behind pain in our life.

Jesus said we would suffer for his namesake. If you know Him, at least you have a source to understand the reason for why and how it can build your faith and your character.

I would like to say God could take away our pain if we just ask and we are instantly healed. However, we have to recognize and surrender to his sovereignty to understand pain.

I have known some people who make threats toward God to save them from their pain or I'll stop believing in You, You are not real. I think, "How dare we demand God to give us life by our terms." Do we hold God hostage or we will deny His existence! Just like the law of gravity - we may not agree with it but it will always work the same way every time. If we step off the edge of a building, disagreeing that it exists, we'll soon find out it is very painful when we splat into the ground. To demand God, answer our prayers the way we like is nothing short of acting like a spoiled child. We all want God to show Himself and prove Himself to us. That is okay; however, we should not demand it. We have to recognize His sovereign authority. A good example is to look at the sin of Job. **As I studied this in the Eye of my pain, I realized I cannot demand of God; rather lean on Him in faith to rescue me in His way, in His timing. So if I prayed Hosanna – Save Now! - I still need to recognize He will save me, but how and when may still involve pain and lots of faith.**

FOOLING OURSELVES IN THE BLACK HOLE

The storms of life test marriages and families more than when life is in a peaceful state. The added stress of a terminal child and dealing with the disease was part of the cause for my first marriage not surviving. It may have fallen apart at some other time. In my case the disease and daily trauma was a trigger that sparked the worst in each spouse. Communication, support, showing love in the way we each needed, and many other needs took a back seat to the disease. Stress was at the highest point when our daughter was terminally ill. The marriage just seemed to echo the lack of future and hope that permeated life during those years. We all have our different points of view on what makes a marriage survive a tragedy and what makes one not survive it. It was like the family black hole - we all were spiraling around and around, further and deeper down into the unknown abyss: wife, husband, mom, dad, daughter, and son. Even extended family, grandmas and grandpas, all lost the dreams, hopes and plans for an expected future.

The abyss of the disease slowly sucked us into its grip of death and hopelessness. Our only hope of escape was our faith, but each faith lifeboat held only a single passenger. The journey of belief is something you go on alone.

Without God's perspective on the pain, there was anger, resentment and unanswered questions. We found ourselves grasping for anything that seemed like a normal life. For example, we went to a parent teacher conference for our terminally ill child of 5 years. She had limited motor skills, a quadriplegic. However, we embraced the parent teacher conference grasping at a feeling of normal. Normally a parent is focused on achievement and how to improve for the future. Right, what future? A normal healthy child's parents would ask, "Is she making friends?" or "Is she doing her homework on time?" How about this one, (Now that I have healthy girls I know it all too well.) "Is she talking too much in class?" – (I would have loved to have that "normal" problem parents complain about!)

We were just there to feel alive and plugged into the world of the living. Maybe a few moments of looking at artwork with our child's name on it helped us feel normal, (even though she had nothing to do with creating it - the teacher did it). We would laugh, smile and tell Nicole what a great job she did with the handprint, the watercolor turkey, the Santa picture, the whatever. Looking back, it is comical to think we were all fooling each other and everybody played along. It felt like we were all on-stage at Saturday Night Live, reading the cue cards and making everyone laugh and be happy. The bitter reality was waiting just off stage on the long car ride home. We lived on the edge of ritual, religion, science, and fantasy. How do you explain the daily grind of dying daily?

LIVING IN LIMBO AND HOPE

Everything was secondary to the disease: birthdays, anniversaries, holidays, the marriage, and the whole family. Everything was less important because someone was dying. Every day we thought, "It could be today." We each coped differently with the terminal illness to find some solid ground to hold onto**. I thought the marriage and family would make it through the disease because of our faith. I thought *I was stronger* than it was. I thought *we were stronger.*** Obviously I had no clue it would get worse before it got better. Everything for the future was put on hold: jobs, careers, challenges, promotions, and special attention for our healthy son. Ambitions took a backseat to the disease. Have you been in a place in life where you felt your life plans were on pause and dreams in a dilemma?

I think our family had **a growing resentment for the disease. It had eaten everything, there was nothing left, and we were all hungry for life.** Honestly, it gets exhausting to keep on loving, caring, and helping someone who is helpless when you yourself are tired and weary.

After a while, help was hard to find and there was no one there to help me. I was so tired of waiting for something to break or get better. I lost patience and thought "anything is better than living in limbo." During the 5-year period after my daughter was diagnosed with the terminal illness, there was no time or energy to think about planning for a bright future **when all you can do is exist in the *now*.** I just thought,

> *"How can I celebrate the next birthday?*
> *How can I celebrate anything normal when our daughter is dying,*
> *Merry Christmas!"*

As long as she was alive I felt there was hope. Maybe that was a false sense of security. I think I was too close to the pain to see how bad it really was. As long as I had my kids to call my own, I could focus my energy on loving them and getting through day-by-day.

With someone to love and live for, God gave me a reason to keep hope alive, because Nicole was alive. I learned to appreciate every breath of life and every blessing no matter how small. I knew that she was headed for heaven, so my concerns were not for her as much as it was for my family and marriage. I saw cracks in the dam of my marriage toward the end and that became my focus. I could not hold it together. I still had hope in my family, my marriage, and my God. I thought He would see me through with my family intact. I thought I deserved to at least keep my family together even if she died. I thought it could not get much worse than losing a child.

ঌ *TAINTED LOVE AND GOOD INTENTIONS* ঌ

I was wrong, it got worse. In a tragedy, the weakness of a marriage is exposed. The song by Soft Cell, **Tainted Love**, describes in simple terms what happened to our marriage:

> "Sometimes I feel I've got to run away... I've got to get away...
> From the pain you drive into the heart of me."

The song goes on to describe a love that had lost its way, how someone runs away from the pain.

We both ran to things to get us out of the pain instead of to each other. I ran to God in a hyper-religious way, because I was trying hard to do good things to save my family.

My ex-wife ran to things she was comfortable with to make the pain go away as well. Either way, we both just wanted the pain to stop.

We both had different ways of coping with our daughter's illness and her inevitable fate. We cooped differently. Seldom did we meet each other's needs. I think that is because only God can meet the needs of parents going through death. I did not want the divorce at first. Toward the end, I accepted it as the best way to move forward. Looking back at the painful experience of the divorce, I remember the judge saying something like this: "Wow, that just happened - your daughter just died after 5 years of an illness. You both need to move on. I'll grant an exception for the divorce for filing less than three months." The rule generally was that you had to wait at least six months for the divorce, between filing and the final judgment. We needed to move on and both just wanted it to be over. Each represented pain to the other and divorce seemed like the best way out of the pain.

My ex-wife and I separated on January 2, 1999, a day after record snowfall barricaded the driveway. She had finally made good on the threat to leave. I was under the impression she was just moving out to get some space. That this would be part of her discovery and recovery process. So with good intentions, I shoveled out the driveway so the moving truck could come in through the snow and haul away all of her precious belongings. She had an apartment her dad helped get so she could start on her journey of discovery. I wonder if the record snowfall was God's way to get her attention,

"Wait, stop, do you really want to do this?"

Snow or no snow she was resolved to make a clean break. Instead of having some of her friends help her, I helped move her out as a sign of good will. Not sure if she knew this or not, but I did not want her friends to bumble through the house at this most sensitive time with the kids in the house. I was embarrassed and ashamed. To me it would have been embarrassing and uncomfortable meeting her new friends as they helped her move out. I thought of the introductions:

"Hello, my name is Ronald, thanks for ruining my life, and what is your name?"

At that time, I thought I would do what I could to mend the relationship, even if it meant shoveling the driveway and helping her take her things. Looking back on it now, I feel very sad. I do not think she intended to hurt anyone, including me. It was just something she had to do. There was so much pain in our house-of-the-dying. I think I just added to her pain in how I dealt with the disease. I was over religious, judgmental, controlling, manipulative, and not very comforting with her choice to get on with her life. That said, I think our combination was toxic. I set off her hot buttons, she set off mine. Still, I thought I had things well under control and I was under the impression she just needed some space.

After she moved out, I saw her one or two times a week, mostly to discuss the kids. She would come by to see them, check on Nicole's health and do what she could to be a good parent. I am not sure if she was trying at the relationship or not, but I tried to give her space.

MY BIG FAT GREEK WEDDING - NOT

My sister was in her early 20's trying to marry the only man she had ever loved. Theo meet her from friends in the neighborhood since she was 15 years old. He hung around the house so much he was more like a fourth brother. Sharon had followed the pattern of our Dad - young love and marrying the first real girlfriend he ever had. She was definitely a daddy's girl, but was having in-law trouble before they were even in-laws! You see Theo is Greek and Sharon is not - that's a big problem. Since Theo's parents did not approve of the marriage idea, Sharon and Theo had to hide their relationship from Theo's parents. For several years they tried to persuade Theo's parents to let them marry and bless their union. Theo bought Sharon a house and had many things ready for their marriage, but his parents' hearts did not soften. So they kept their relationship secret from Theo's parents.

I had the day off work for the MLK Holiday a few weeks after my ex-wife left. I thought things were going well with the new arrangement: We were not arguing, she would come by and see the kids when she could and she seemed happy. I thought we could have breakfast together and discuss plans since I had the day off. On my way to her home I learned she did not want to be married to me any longer. I finally realized our marriage was over. I was beside myself. Crushed and not sure what to do next, I needed someone to talk to. Most people were busy at work. But I could always rely on my sister, if she was home, so I gave her a call. I wondered what to do with the rest of my day off... the rest of my life....my family's life. I looked for someone to call for help and share my awfulness, maybe find some solace. I called my sister and she answered the phone. I thought to myself,

"Thank God she answered the phone."

Sharon answered the phone and was there for me like always, to help me feel better. I was grateful for my close family support, something not everyone is blessed with. She informed me she was busy that day getting married! Theo had enough of being pushed around by his parents and they were going to elope. She offered that I come with them and be their witness. Thinking of it now, they were my witness, witnesses of my heart breaking, when their hearts were being joined together. I said "yes," I would love to go with them.

With my heart breaking, their hearts were healing. I took this as a sign that God was in control and He held my heart when it was breaking.

☙ *JUSTICE AND FREEDOM FOR ALL* ☙

Not only did I want to go, I needed to go with my sister. **This was my greatest distraction in a time of greatest heartbreak.**

Thanks, little sis! And Theo! I was excited for the two of them. **In the middle of the realization my marriage was over, my sister's was just beginning. Literally, the same day, the same moment.** What an odd paradox. On the way to the courthouse, I was on the phone with my ex-wife trying to understand what she was doing.

While on the way to the Justice of the Peace, I was trying to find justice and peace for why she was ending our marriage.

I told her what Sharon was doing, expecting her to be happy for them, not realizing the oddness of my thoughts. I was desperate for any glimpse of hope. After I got off the phone with her, I realized my hope was right there in the car with me, in my family and friends who would help pick me up off the emotional floor and help me get to my new normal. Truly, God had arranged the plans that day.

We had a wonderful time as we enjoyed the day together. What a way to celebrate Martin Luther King Day, a way I will never forget. Isn't that what the man symbolizes? Justice and Freedom for all. Sharon was standing up for the oppression of her in-laws. My wife was breaking free of the chains of marriage to get her freedom. Later**, I came to understand how good God was to send me support, right when I needed it as a sign**. I felt a peace in finding out my marriage was over when Sharon's was just beginning and I knew God would make a way to meet my needs. It was then I saw the first glimmer of the light at the end of the tunnel. I would make it through this storm. Life would go on for me, somehow, someway. This is not just a cruel joke. I felt like I had no time to grieve, but just enough time to take it in and move on. God knew I needed to move on to my sister's marriage and the welcome support of those who cared for me.

KEEP MOVING THROUGH THE STORM

In those crazy times, when my family was falling apart, I felt as if I was going through hell but never alone. I knew Christ was there with me. In that moment, I felt a quickening to just keep moving. I was committed to keeping my faith even if it meant being single again, regardless of who did or did not supported me. I needed to stand on God's Word, His people, and those He sent into my life who would be there for me. When I was in the Eye of the Storm I am reminded of the song by Rodney Atkins, **If You're Going Through Hell**. The basic theme to the song is to keep on moving through the pain, keep on doing what you can do to get through and get out of it. Do not make too much of a fuss, do not make a lot of noise as to wake the devil.

> "If you're goin' through hell keep on going, Don't slow down, if you're scared don't show it...Angels everywhere, holdin' out a hand to pull you back up on your feet"

The song is comical in a way, but filled with practical advice.

Much of our recovery from storms depends on our heart attitude. How will you see your past, your present, and your future? There are angels and there are demons watching to see what you will do. The choice is yours: will you chose to be blessed or will you stay knocked down?

As we learned earlier in this chapter faith is a fight and a race. Keep running and keep fighting. The song then suggests, since you are knocked down on your knees, you might as well pray and see what will happen.

"S" SHORTCUT TO P.A.S. THROUGH THE STORM

We already learned that the "P" and "A" are for Prayer and Accountability, and now in chapter 6 we discussed the "S" shortcut is for "Sovereign God."

We can faithfully depend in His sovereign plan to work for our good and learn our only hope is in His sovereignty.

I think of our relationship to God much like the marriage relationship; we are told to accept our spouse for better or worse. We all can praise God when things are going "For Better" and our faith life boat is humming along calm seas. In Gods sovereignty, we need to stay faithful to our relationship with Jesus, even when it is difficult. From this chapter we have learned some ways to endure life in the storms of "for worse." We build our faith in these times and have no other choice when life is the darkest storms. Then we can find our hope, if we only believe!

Secret 3

Restore the Reason

Chapter 7

Get Bitter or get Better

"Let today be the day you stop being haunted by the ghost of yesterday. Holding a grudge & harboring anger/ resentment is poison to the soul. Get even with people... but not those who have hurt us, forget them, instead get even with those who have helped us."

Steve Maraboli

ACCEPTANCE LEADS TO HEALING

My story about Nicole is very similar to other stories of someone losing a child to childhood disease. Maybe you have lost a child or someone you love. Eventually we all have to face how we are going to handle death, our own or one of those we love. I think the biggest thing we struggle with is when we do not get what we think is fair. We think death for an older person is fairer than death for a young person, 80 years old vs. 8 years old. One thing we learn if we are observers of life - people die at all ages. But we've been indoctrinated to be fair.

> *"Johnny share your crayons with Susie...."*

...Because that would be fair, we tell our children. Our institutions teach us to be fair.

> *"Don't only bring one cupcake to share with your friend, bring enough for the whole class because that's fair."*
> *"Take Turns"* ... and so on....

As we grow up we learn that in the real world nothing is fair - class, environments, gifts, and abilities. Life is anything but fair. Even the Kingdom of God is not fair, so why would we think that life on earth should be fair. In Matthew 20, Jesus explains how the Kingdom of God is like a farmer who pays his workers the same wage no matter when they started working for him. Some worked one hour and some worked all day. You see, the farmer makes an individual deal with each worker and may be different. The plan God has for each of us is our deal as we labor on earth and no two experience is the same.

God has a Deal made just for you; It's the plan He has for you to follow and the cross He wants you to bear and your reason.

God does the same for us in this life. Each of us is guaranteed nothing. Each day is a gift from God and only He knows when our time is up. What we get out of life depends on how we see God. Emily Rapp wrote a book about her son, Ronan, who contracted the fatal disease *Tay-Sachs*. She recounts it in her book: **The Still Point of a Turning World**:

"This is a love story which, like all great love stories, is ultimately a story of loss. On January 10, 2011, my husband, Rick, & I received the worst possible news that our son Ronan then 9 months old had Tay Sachs disease, a rare, progressive, and always fatal condition with no treatment and no cure."

In this book she retells the cruelties of this disease and the God that allowed it. She questions if He exists.

While we all wrestle with blame, sometimes our grief blinds us to the reason that is beyond our understanding.

The Bible speaks about our understanding being not the same as God's. It claims our heart is deceitful... and we cannot trust it. It also explains our inability to understand the events in life as we only see through a veil, dimly. When we put our faith in God during the storm, we learn we can depend on God for comfort and understanding. At the same time, we can question and learn to trust Him for the reason why it happens.

The healing begins when we let go of the unknown and accept what is known. In time, we find the reasons to go on to greater purpose.

Instead of blaming God and growing in our bitterness, we can learn to seek His reasons for the scars of our life. Even though we may not understand the storms, it is only through the cross of pain and suffering can we know the joys of heaven and its higher purpose of life. **Heaven is for Real** is a story about a country pastor wrestling with the reasons for his storms. The main character, Todd has a climactic moment as he shares his anger with God. He is tired of how hard his life is and how he just has to accept it. Then Todd tells God He is crossing the line for him to take his son. Later in the story, the doctors describe his son's survival as a miracle as he survives the operation and eventually makes a full recovery. After his son survives Todd begins to search for answers. Why did this happen? Why did they have to go through all that pain? He concludes the answer is in his son's revelations while in heaven, the things he saw, most importantly - heaven is real. The bottom line from the movie –

there are reasons why bad things happen because God uses them to reveal himself, His purposes, and His glory to the world.

Have there been bad things happened in your life, things God used in your life? When something bad happens God becomes an easy target for our anger. Are we so quick to blame Him for the good things? We can become bitter in our pride and arrogance. We think we know what is best for our life and do not want to be told we are wrong. Children and teenagers often blame their parents for their problems because they represent God's authority. We easily praise God for the good things but the Christian worldview is to praise God for both good and bad. Romans 8:28 says:

> *"And we know that in all things God works for the good of those who love him, who have been called according to his purpose."* (NIV)

God's plan is to use all things to help us grow. That is His plan. Our journey to heaven and eternity starts the moment we recognize Christ as Savior. Then we start the education journey of growing into the person we were born to be. All along we can have assurance - heaven is awaiting our future. Paul reminds us in this verse:

"...do not forget those we know that have died with Christ will be raised again." (1Thess 4:13)

This perspective helps put our storms into perspective, even life and death.

ঌ *STORMS MAKE US LOOK UP* ঌ

Bad things happen. Many times they are the only way God can get our attention, to drive us to our knees, to call to Him in prayer. Recently a storm passed by and I thought of this idea as we moved to the basement for shelter. "It is time to strap on the prayer gear," I thought. Many times in our busy lives God and prayer are afterthoughts. Sometimes when there is no hope, when we've tried everything else, then we run to God in prayer. The storms cause us to recognize God. Then we realize He has reasons why these things happen even though I may not like or understand it. When I was a child and my parents told me to do things I did not want to do, I'd rebel in any way possible. It's the same thing when we grow up. We have bad things happen to us or things don't go our way. As a child, we experienced punishment as a storm that corrects us and makes us become obedient. As an adult, storms play the correcting role in our lives.

It is only in accepting the storms for the purpose of correcting and seeing God clearly that we recognize His plan of restoration and our future of an eternity in heaven.

I wish it were not so, but it serves as a reminder that we need God. If I'm smart, I will not wait for storms to go to God.

If I am wise, I will seek Him daily and not wait for the flood to buy flood insurance. When I am communicating more often with God, it helps me remember He is in control. It gives me peace in a stress-filled life. It causes me to remember God is working all things for my good and He is not finished with me yet. Even in the worst-case scenario of death, Paul says 'to live is Christ and to die is gain.' I just need to **focus on my purpose. Then God gives me His strength to overcome tragedy and fears.** The outcome of any storm is up to God. The eternal perspective is my motivator, causing me to remember my purpose and focus on why I'm here and my God-given calling. For about 3 years with my terminally ill child, I prayed every night for her that she soon would be home in heaven. When death is so near, heaven seems close as well. In realizing heaven in the everyday things of life, we can remember reasons to live life to the fullest every day.

༄ *DADDY SHE NEVER SAID – RESTORED* ༄

The death of my daughter and the divorce made me feel that my life was in a burned-up heap. I asked God to give me a sign that He was still with me, that He would allow my terminally ill daughter to say daddy. Well, I never heard those words from her, never thought I would. I eventually did – but from my third daughter. While I was in the moment of the disease, I did not understand what God's purpose was in my storm but I knew I had to lean on Him and trust Him even when I could not see Him. In my pain, I did one thing right that is described in Joel 2:12 – 13 (NAS):

> "Even now," declares the Lord,
>   "return to me with all your heart,
>   with fasting and weeping and mourning."
> Rend your heart
>   and not your garments.
> Return to the Lord your God,
>   for he is gracious and compassionate,

I realized later, only when I learned to go to my prayer closet regularly, that God had pointed the way out of my storms. As I learn to seek God and His answers for why they happened, I now realize God restored beauty from my ashes. I had lost years of life through the heartache of disease, death, and divorce. And now in the process of seeking God I found the blessings revealed to me. Much like the verse from Joel:

> *And I will restore to you the years that the locust hath eaten, the cankerworm, and the caterpillar, and the palmerworm, my great army which I sent among you."* (Joel 2:25 NSV)

In this story from the Old Testament, the prophet Joel was relaying a message to the Israelites. They had turned their backs on God and His ways and had let sin run their day-to-day lives. God sent a storm of locust to destroy all they had and their hope. Now after they turned away from sin and their lives back to God, He promised to restore to them all they had lost. I am not blaming any of my actions per se on my daughter dying; rather, just sin in the broader sense. It is the sin in the world, the sin in my life, and sin in the form of the disease that took my daughter's life. In addition, God had a plan that He allowed this terrible thing to happen. I feel it is as if God said to me:

> *"And I will restore to you the years that sin hath eaten, the disease, the death, and the divorce, my great army which I sent among you.*

Can you think of storms of God's army that have happened in your life? God has a reason why they happen. You may not understand them, like them, or even grasp why a loving God would do this, but you are not supposed to! However, you are supposed to look to God, his word and trust His sovereign plan, not always understand it. I wrestled with the reason my first daughter died, never getting even the smallest of signs of God's presence, His allowing my daughter to say "Daddy;" however,

God showed me His reason, when I began to let go of my "Why?" and started seeking for His "What Now?"

Slowly my faith became stronger and God blessed me for the year's sin had stolen. Then I had more than a daughter who said, "Daddy." I learned the true meaning of me saying, "Daddy" to my Heavenly Father Who showers His children with good gifts. Only by letting go of the "why?" can we get through our storms with our faith intact and find our reasons to go on to Gods blessings.

When our heart learns to ask "What now?" we find out God's purpose is to use the storms to give Him the glory through the power of the transformative cross.

What should you do now that the storm has affected your life? God says through the prophet in Isaiah:

> *"To all who mourn in Israel, they will give a crown of beauty for Ashes, a joyous blessing instead of morning, festive praise instead of despair. In their righteousness, he will be like great oaks that the Lord has planted for His own glory."* (Isaiah 61:3, NLT)

That's it - the transformation of your storm into His glory. When everything is falling down around us we have the hope of Christ and eternity as our reason, then coming out victorious when it does not make sense.

That's exactly when God can use us, when everything in our life is senseless. Even though I do not understand it, the fact remains: if my first daughter had not died I would not have the two daughters I currently have. They serve as a reminder of my life's beauty from ashes.

❧ *THE DAUGHTERS OF SACRIFICE, BLESSING, AND PROMISE* ❧

All right, now that I have just said let go of the "Why?" there is a time to pick it up again, in light of God's word. Many times the storms teach us important things about God's character and what He wants us to learn. Each of my daughters has taught me something about God.

- My first daughter taught me about **sacrifice**.
- My second daughter taught me about **blessing**,
- and my third daughter taught me about **promises**.

They all represent parts of my learning who God is because of my storms. They help me understand ***why*** God gave them to me and the reason God planned for me to learn from each of them. When I think of the word daughter – it means to me a beautiful harvest or fruit of my labor, (because they are a lot of work!) In the following "daughters" are examples try to see your storms as the labor of God's working in your heart to bring about these blessings in your life.

DAUGHTER OF SACRIFICE:

The perfect lamb, God's own son, the spotless one. Jesus was that sacrifice for all mankind. My daughter showed me a glimpse of what God went through. Even with all the power, He suffered terrible pain when He sacrificed Jesus, who did no wrong. Also when I think of the vain pursuits of this life and compare it to Heaven and the eternal Kingdom of God, I realize my loss of a parent's dreams, my hopes, and my plans for my first daughter.

The sacrifice is necessary to see the blessings that wait just beyond them.

Without Nicole's sacrifice, I could not have learned many valuable lessons to be a better man and father. I would never have meet my stepdaughter,

Katrina and current wife, or have a second born daughter, Genevieve. Beyond these tangible blessings,

God reveals the higher reasons for storms that build Christ-like character that gives God the glory in our life.

Without this first daughter of sacrifice, there cannot be a daughter of blessing and daughter of promise. When you get the revelation of why God has given you your storms, you want to find your reason to praise Him and give Him the glory. But it all starts with sacrifice. For each of us, that is what Jesus did on the cross. Now we can have blessings and His promises - if we chose to seek them! How else can God restore what sin has stolen if nothing was stolen? The pain of sacrifice is to show us that our sin separates us from God. My first daughter sacrificed her life because of sin in the world. This providence and pain allowed me to be father to Katrina who desperately wanted a daddy in her life. Jesus is that sacrifice for the whole world so that we can have His blessings and promises.

DAUGHTER OF BLESSING:

I believe God gave me a daughter of blessing in my stepdaughter who was the same age as my first daughter would have been.

Blessings are the times when God works on my behalf and blesses me in spite of my sin, eventually restoring a right heart within me.

At times I thought of her as the daughter of rebelliousness. But I've come to realize this is how I am as well. God blesses us when we turn from our sin. There are times when I want my own way instead of pleasing God. But thankfully I am able to turn to Him for correction and forgiveness. 1st Peter 5:10 says:

"And the God of all grace, who called you to his eternal glory in Christ, after you have suffered a little while, will himself restore you and make you strong, firm, and steadfast."

I take this to heart - that after my heart was turned toward Him and my suffering was over, He established me by blessing me with a daughter the same age as the one I had lost. I did not have to wait 7 years to get to experience a 7 yr. old.

Just as Abraham took matters into his own hands to have a child from his concubine, God foreknew my decisions would lead Katrina to be my daughter, even though she was not in my original plans. Her legal parents planned for her and I was blessed with her after enduring the death of my 1st born daughter. **This pain enabled me to have more love and appreciation for my daughters.** The pain of losing a daughter made me appreciate what I had in her and fight that much harder to make our relationship work. Only God could have planned it that way! He made extra room in my heart for her because of my loss.

I found my second daughter only after I recommitted my life to God only the night before. I believed this was a sign of blessings from God, and I gave Him the glory. Whenever I had a challenge in my relationship with my stepdaughter, I remembered how God gave her to me as a blessing and how full of joy I was to have her in my life.

When I remember her as a blessing, it helps me to believe God's promises to restore what sin destroyed - my sin. That leads me to the future of a life depending on His promises every day.

DAUGHTER OF PROMISE:

I never asked God for another daughter after the death of my first daughter. God just knew my pain and my loss. I did, however feel He would bless me if I committed my ways to Him. He would keep His promises. Even though

I had divorced and remarried, he gave me the privilege and responsibility to have a daughter again, a second chance. Many places in the Bible God gives us a second chance, a chance for us to see His mercy and experience His joy. I struggled for years trying to accept Gods message, but finally believed it as a sign of God's promises. Maybe it was my doubt that God could deliver on His promise and I thought,

"God would not message me in this way, it is just a coincidence,"

After some soul searching and many years of life with both daughters, I realized God was showing me both blessings and His promises in my daughters.

As I sought to know Him more, He revealed himself to me in my daughters. Katrina has been saved from many bad choices in life and is enjoying some restoration herself, not only with God but also to us, her family. She impacts and connects all of us, her step-brother, Zac, and her half-sister Gen. We all have our place in the family and we realize how important we are to one another.

Another outcome of storms is a new appreciation for the brevity of life and we can learn to be good to and encourage each other. Holding on to Gods promises leads to answered prayers and blessings.

In Genesis, Chapter 12, Abraham's story of faith is told. Because he kept his faith in God's promises, God changed his heart and changed the world.

Abraham's perseverance and tenacity to hold on tightly to God's promises opened the door for God to bless Him.

God promised to make him a great nation began the moment Abraham believed in God. Just like us when we come to God for salvation - it starts out with a great promise, salvation. But then the trials and storms start and our faith is tested. What would your life be like if you hold tightly to God's promises in your life's storms? God promises to bless you if you hold on to your faith in your storms.

REALIZE BEING RESTORED

January 2, 1999 saw one of the biggest snowstorms of recent history in southeast Michigan. That was also moving day for my ex-wife. She was leaving our marriage of 9 plus years. It was the pinnacle of many numerous fights and unhappiness from many sources. The future was unknown as to what would happen to our terminally ill daughter and we made it sound like a good thing to our son, that mom was going to have a cool, new place he could visit and have fun. As I shoveled snow so the truck could make it in the driveway, I felt some strength that we were moving in a direction. Not my best choice, but at least it was movement. After many years of disease and talk of divorce, now something was finally happening. As I reluctantly packed the truck I thought "this furniture is not coming back." Even though she told me it was just a trial separation, I knew it was the beginning of the end.

Some thought I was crazy and out of my mind. If she wants out, let her do it own her own! But I was helping her because I was starting to see my fault, my sin. I was starting to see that these bad things happening in my life because I was not the best husband. I felt a little like I deserved this because I was coming to realize why she was leaving. It was not only the reason for her pain, her not being able to live with me. It was also all about God teaching me something that I needed to see, the pain I caused her. This is the same pain each of our sins cause others by not following God's plan for our life.

This was the beginning of my wakeup call, but also the beginning of my restoration. Realizing my wrong was the first step in my healing.

Sometimes we need a crisis event to shake us to our core in order to get our attention. The next waypoint in being restored happened in the fabric of the tear-stained closet, where I wrestled with God on why He had taken my girls from me.

After wrestling with an angel, comparing myself to Job, humbling myself before God, and repenting of my part in the devastation, a light bulb thought turned on: FIND YOUR REASON.

As I picked myself up from the closet floor, I began to feel hungry again. It was late in the evening, only fast food was open and I needed to get some fresh air. So I wandered out to grab a burger. On the way back home I summarized the blessings that remained after the storm. I was still a dad to my wonderful son, I had a decent job, and I had a nice house. I could learn to live life differently, a life of just the boys, because that is what I now had in my new reality. Thus it began, my coming to the realization God would fill in the holes in my life. I could change, I would need to change.

I needed to learn to trust God again in a completely new way. He would restore my faith and hope now that love had gone away.

I have to admit; I was down on myself. My family had disintegrated in front of me and I needed to focus on what I did have. Just as God told Moses to use what he had in his hands to rescue the Israelites from Egyptian bondage, I had to use what I still had to be what God needed me to be.

Moses had a staff, I had my son. What better reason could there be for me to become a better man?

My son Zachary. At that time, he was 8 years old and probably wondering,

"'what bomb just dropped on my family?'

I'd found my reason to stay strong. His cute little smile – he has my dimples.

His love provided the positive vibes, letting me know I was still of value to someone who loved me. For a while this kept me on the right track toward recovery. He paved the way for future struggles and God's lessons for me to learn and grown more in His grace.

BECOMING WHO I'M SUPPOSED TO BE

Are we human beings on a spiritual journey?

When you discover you are a spiritual being, then the emphasis changes to who you really are.

We are spiritual beings on a human journey.

This means the eternal Spirit is in the driver's seat of your life. You see everything through that spiritual lens, with heaven and eternal goals being lived out while on our human journey.

The emphasis in life is then placed on the spiritual life ruling the core of our human self. One of the most important emotional drivers in life is that of being loved. We often see this lived out when our emotional and physical needs are met. However, as spiritual beings, they can only be truly met by remembering we are spiritual beings on a human journey. This song by

Brandon Heath is a great reminder of what love is all about. **<u>I'm Not Who I Was</u>**

> *"I used to be mad at you, a little on the hurt side too. But I'm not who I was.*
> *I found my way around, to forgiving you - some time ago ..."*

The song reminisces about love and what love used to be like; it starts to wallow in self-pity, wondering if she ever loved him. **Maybe because real love is the kind of love the Bible speaks of and is not possible without God at the heart of a couple's love.** In love if God is not present to hold it together, there are winners and losers. He gets his way; she gets her way. She wants to change him. He wants to do his own thing. Whoever manipulates "love" is the winner...and on goes the relationship without God. In contrast, God's love is different as seen in a marriage relationship.

He goes on in the song to discuss what love is really all about - *amazing grace*. In addition, the most amazing thing we get to do is give it out to others. Once you realize the truth about love and how much God's kind of love is **real love**, then you can recognize the world's "fake" love and apply God's design to make it right. This helps me when I look back in my life where I have had failed relationships, along with the associated hurts, and not have bad feelings, rather a new understanding. His love is amazing grace; it sacrifices self for the good of others. Realizing this task takes worldly love and flips it on its head. Where it used to be all about me, is now all about others and God's will. Love is really about God's amazing grace extended toward each of us, then how you and I can show that grace to others.

CHANGED FOR THE BETTER

I realized then that even though I had tried to be an involved dad in Zac's life, I hadn't been as involved and responsible with his mom - I let everything fall on her shoulders. Now with my new focus in life, I started to be a more dependable dad. I became a den leader for my son in Cub

Scouts and a leader in the church kid's program, AWANA. I began to balance things with his mom and get help from our neighbors, Bill and Gina, when I had to work late. The focus now became 'what can I do with what God has given me?' It also became 'how can I give the glory to God where I am right now as a single dad.' I was not perfect in my efforts, but now I got the picture and stopped being a by-stander parent. Now I got in the game.

I took the *Divorce Care* class at my church, realizing many things I had done wrong in my marriage disintegration. I stopped beating myself up but also realized my part. My final realization – I had been just plain selfish. I thought I just loved her too much; but I came to realize it was not real love, rather a carnal self-centered view of what a wife is for. I only thought about my agenda, my goals, my desires, and my dreams. I was a loud personality that did not show enough concern for her pain. For this, I am truly sorry she went through those hard times. Do not get me wrong, I was not an extremely horrible husband in the typical fashion. I worked hard, I did not cheat on her, I went to church, etc.... My part in the breakup could be summed up in a simple term - selfishness.

I was not sensitive to her well-being. This may have meant I would have had to sacrifice my fun times for just being alone with her and being quiet. That is the opposite of me. I did not allow those time where she could set the agenda, do her thing, and feel free within the marriage. I realize now that we all have a different temperament and need to feel love in different ways. Some need more affection, some want less. Some want loud things, some like quiet contemplation. I needed to learn to listen better.

Everyone that goes through divorce can grow more mature as we analyze our part in light of Gods word.

Marriage is the ultimate view of God's love for the world and if it is not done with a self-less heart, then it is wrong and the first crisis of faith will cause each spouse to hunker down in his or her vices. My vise was very simple but hidden. It was hidden in my righteousness – myself. We all hide as an escape. My escape was just me! I thought I was strong enough, good enough, and righteous enough that I was impervious to the needs, feelings, wants, and desires of those around me. There was a healthy amount of ego, perhaps too much, and I did not see to the needs of others. I missed concern for others because I was so busy saving the world my way. Today I still think I have many good ideas on how to fix something, do a project, or my opinion is a good one.

However, I remind myself it is not important to get my way if I hurt others I love along the way. I am still learning this in my current marriage. Many times I pray to get "*me*" out of the way, not allowing my way unless my wife is on board with the decision. That is what it means to be married, be submissive to one another, to show love. It grieves me I am so thickheaded, but I am thankful that at least now my eyes are open and I see what I need to be. This is the gift of girls in my life. They will squeeze all of the selfishness right out of me. Many of my feelings are expressed in this song **Changed** by Rascal Flats:

> *"Back slid my way into that place where souls get lost*
> *I'm changed for the better.... More smiles, less bitter"*

The song goes on to say how the mistakes in life can bring about true change if we drop to our knees and pray, admitting our wrongs to God, the Father. After this confession time, you can now see who you truly are and move forward into the reality of changes that need to take place. Learning the truth about myself meant I could learn to be honest about who I am and the changes I needed, and to live in peace and harmony in my world.

Maybe it is in just the last couple years since my stepdaughter, Katrina left the house that I realize how blessed I am. She's not perfect and I'm not perfect, but we learned to accept each other and our faults. If I had not gone through the storms of 3 "D" s I would not have as much patience and endurance to love and pursue a relationship with her. I never would have had her. I keep reminding her I loved her first. It's much like how God loved us first so much that he sent Jesus. I think I tried so hard with Katrina. Stepdaughters are hard to work into a blended family and to get over all of the drama and trauma from the real dad gets sticky quickly. I believe she was sent into my life as an answer to prayer, but also as a way to show me God's restoration to us. I had no clue what I was doing when I asked God for daughters. It was much more difficult than I thought it would be, not to mention needing to see my need to grow spiritually to be the kind of dad they need. Blessings and growth go together. They lead to the man I am now. Just like the song **Changed**, I'm a better man because of them. All of this in my life and my two beautiful daughters - I have Nicole to thank as she sacrificed her life so that my eyes would be opened and I would become the man God intended me to be. I think it really stinks; it's not fair she had to die, but I do see something good came out of it. I do not think any of it would've happened if I held onto my pain, remaining bitter toward God for her death. Even if I did have a stepdaughter at some point, I would not have been able to love her without an open heart of forgiveness for the pain that was sure to come my way. By my internal perspective in the big scheme of life, Nicole saved her two sisters and she's in heaven in a perfect place. Thanks, Nicole, I love you, Daddy.

Chapter 8

Rescue the Reason

It was men who stopped slavery. It was men who ran up the stairs in the Twin Towers to rescue people. It was men who gave up their seats on the lifeboats of the Titanic. Men are made to take risks and live passionately on behalf of others.

John Eldredge

⅋ *RESCUE THE LOST SHEEP* ⅋

Jeff Stimpson, one of my pastors, said,

> *"Sometimes you have a chance when you least expected it."* He continued, *"In my profession, I'm always looking for lost souls."*

He is looking wherever he goes. He was out shopping at an outlet mall with his wife, more appropriately he was holding down a bench outside the stores in the husband's pit stop area. His goal of shopping was that of a supportive, giving husband, out shopping with his wife. He intended this to be a boring affair, downtime, but sacrificing for the good of the family! '*Taking one for the team*' he calls it.

As a good searcher of lost souls is, He was keenly aware and observant of his surroundings. Even though he was not in the shopping game, he was literally sitting on the bench; he liked watching the game. From his vantage point in midfield, he noticed all the shoppers, busy with their packages, bags, and agendas, hurrying from place to place in their own little shopping bubbles. Nobody noticed each other or even connected in a noticeable way as they floated past each other.

In the midst of the holiday hassle, Jeff noticed a horrified little Asian girl with an obviously lost look on her face. Since Jeff was keeping track of the shopping game very well from his seat at the 50-yard line, he also noticed a maddened Asian mother, waving her arms and screaming in a foreign dialect. She was obviously upset about something. When he looked back at the little girl, he instantly saw the resemblance and ran toward the little girl. He quickly but gently guided the lost little lamb to her mother. He was able to reunite the two because he was aware of helpless and lost people. What would have happened if Jeff had not been watching, then seeing the frantic mother, seeing the lost daughter and putting the two together?

God can only use you if you are looking for His lost sheep. Are you looking for Jesus' lost lambs in your life?

Or are you floating by in your own bubble?

Jesus rescued the one lost sheep from a fold of one hundred. He wants us to not only search for lost sheep but also to feed His sheep. Are you a seeker of lost sheep? Are you a rescuer of lost sheep? Maybe you are a feeder of His lost sheep. Feeding His lost sheep could be something as simple as sharing your story, what God has done for you. Feeding God's lost sheep was the main driver for me writing this book. One day I realized I was not brought through storms just to keep the blessings all to myself. Maybe my story connects with you. Maybe your story can connect with someone else. Part of your blessing is in sharing your story that will connect with someone else, not to mention the joy that comes from helping others. When you share with others you realize the reason for rescuing others the way Jesus rescued you.

At times, all of us are like lost children searching for hope when we are lost in the storms of life. You can be a blessing to others by being alert and looking for life's lost souls.

THE LOST GIRLS

My mom and dad are my heroes because they've always been looking for lost souls. I think they can relate to those who are lost because they both had rough childhood beginnings and found Jesus in the storm of their life: Raising 5 children with no support. My parents took-in my cousin, Mary, to live with them when she was only 6 years old. Her mother had health issues and her dad had run off. That left my parents as the only close family who could take her in. She was like an instant sister to me the day she showed up. I did not know the complications involved, but I know my parents rescued her from a life in foster homes and who knows what other trials she could have had.

Things were seemingly normal until she hit her teenage years. Boys started noticing her in the neighborhood and at school. She got involved with the wrong crowd. Mary wanted a closer relationship with her father as she began to discover who he was. That left her discontented with her identity. She kept looking for that close father figure relationship. I think it safe to say, she never quite got what she was looking for at our home. So she decided to run away to a friend's house. After life "on the lam" for a couple of days, she ended up back home with us. I am sure my parents thought the trials were over and everything would return to normal when she came back home. In reality, this was just the beginning off my cousin's storms and her journey to find happiness. I'm sure she would say she had valid reasons why she ran away. She would say, "*I was treated unfairly,*" not like a normal daughter. From my understanding that was true, there were thing that may have hurt her feelings. The details of these issues are not important. What is important - know you are loved unconditionally with a father's love. I think my dad did his best to love her and from my vantage point, he showed her as much love as he showed us three boys. Then along came our little sister. My dad finally had his girl, Mary was about 10 years old at that time. As the growing needs of a baby girl began to crowd out limited parental resources, I could see Mary striving to find love from parents who were doing the best they could. She eventually ran away for good at the age of 15.

For 2 years, our family ached from the loss of Mary, wondering what had happened to her. From time to time, we would hear news about her. Once she was in Texas with a man twice her age, she was alive and safe. For now, that was good enough for my parents. They could sleep at night knowing she was alive and doing the best she could. Much later, in her twenties, we saw her when she rekindled her relationship with our family. My parents had limited involvement with her over the next few years. Eventually they lost touch and Mary drifted out of our life. The relationship ended "strained" at best. No one really knows why there was never reconciliation with Mary, my parents, and the rest of the family. Maybe one day this will change and there will be acceptance and appreciation for the roles each played in one another's life. For now, I am thankful that my parents did the right thing. We had many happy memories and good times with Mary as part of our family; that is until she started looking for more love than our family could give her.

When my stepdaughter Katrina entered my life, things were going well when she was a little girl. But as she grew into her teenage years, she yearned for more love than any father could provide. It reminded me of Mary. I tried to do everything I could to make her feel like a real daughter and part of the family. In addition, as irony would have it, Katrina was the same age Mary was when a baby girl entered the home; they were both 10 years old. As I learned the love of a father to a daughter with my baby, I thought of how Katrina must feel. It also reminded me of my cousin Mary when my sister Sharon was born, how she must have felt very similar. I realize from my situation growing up with Mary that she needed more love and reassurance then a natural born daughter. They need extra reassurance that a step dad will love them unconditionally the way Christ gave His life for the church. To make matters more complicated, stepdaughters have a trust issue. I learned this with Katrina, that she had her own issues to work out and I needed to give her grace to allow me to work out my issues, trying to love her as best as I could. Katrina started going down the same road that Mary went down.

I was faced with the same issues that my father faced trying to love a rebellious runaway stepdaughter in the midst of raising my own natural born daughter.

My stepdaughter got to see the natural love between my baby girl - Genevieve and the love she never had and missed out on. I could see the jealousy and the hurt. From the age of 15 through 18, she ran away from home several times and there were numerous days when we didn't know where she was. To be blunt, she put us through hell. There is no worse ache than a parent's heartbreak when they don't know if their child is alive or dead. My mind flashed back to my cousin Mary and the pain my family felt when she was missing in action. My emotions were also stirred up remembering the fatal feelings of my terminally ill first daughter. It was that helpless feeling when there is nothing you can do but wait.

This was a time when my wife and I clung together to God in prayer. We also looked to the Bible for wisdom as I remembered the lessons I learned in my past storms where I had to *Endure the Eye!*

It was during those times of pain and not knowing where she was that God worked on me. He used this storm for my good even though I doubted him. I cried out to Him in my pain anyway. He helped me have more love and forgiveness for when she was ready to come back home. Why is it when you lose someone you love, you forget all of the wrongs they did just because you love them so much? **In the end I realized this was part of the plan so that I would learn the love God has for all of us, and that I could have that same love for her.**

ঌ *HIS GRACE - MY MISSION, LARGER THAN MY LIFE* ঌ

The paradox was, she had a dad but he was on the other side of the country. However, I was here with her.

I saw loving Katrina as a blessing, an opportunity, a chance to live a mission larger than my life: to love her when she's being unlovely, to love her with Christ love when my love runs out of strength.

As I went through my struggles with Katrina, I realized my mission: it was simple to love her as God loves us, unconditionally. You see, God prepared me for everything I went through with Mary and with Nicole. I knew the recipe was the same, to love the lost and hurting souls. Thank God, He prepared me and gave me strength to be able to withstand her rebellion.

I realized she was a lost soul searching for her heavenly Father taking her frustration out on me.

That's what she needed and that's what all of us need. To become all that God intends us to be He teaches us through those difficult relationships in our lives. The lesson I learned was that I am as lost as she was and my pride stops me from loving unconditionally, so I need God's grace more than her.

It is only when I set my ego aside and realize what a helpless sinner I truly am, that I can love as Christ intends.

It's scary to think how many times I blew it, argued, and let stupid issues come between us. However, I knew my mission was to reconcile no matter how many times I had to say sorry to Katrina or forgive her for something. I wanted her to know that I would bury my pride and my selfishness and do whatever it takes to show she is important and loved.

It was hard work and at times a sacrifice, but because I had lost my first girl, I had extra strength from God to help me not lose my second girl.

I always saw her as a gift from God sent into my life at a time when I needed her the most. She was my blessing.

- Would it help your relationship struggles if you saw them as a blessing from God?
- Would it change the way you interact with them?
- Would it help you see them in a different light?

God designed people into your life to refine your character, to make you strong enough to withstand the storms in your life. 2 Corinthians 12:9 explains my point - *Each time he said,*

> *"My grace is all you need. My power works best in weakness." So now I am glad to boast about my weaknesses, so that the power of Christ can work through me."*

In our spiritual life, everything we naturally think is strength is actually a weakness spiritually. When I have a difficult relationship, I should realize God is using this difficult circumstance, through this person to refine my character and become stronger in Christ. Most of us want to run away from the area in which we are the weakest. We are tempted to blame the storms or blame the person with whom we have an issue and the conflict continues. God will keep the conflict in our life until we pass the test. Can we understand God is using this storm to refine us? In chapter 6, I mentioned the section about –

"Your Cross is Your Curriculum."

Well, guess what? When storms come, its test time.

When you see your loss through the lens of the cross, you learn to love with the Father's heart.

I eventually got around to seeing that my weaknesses are where I need to be more like Christ in my relationship with Katrina. Once I saw my relationship through this lens, our relationship was on the road to healing.

I always wanted to keep my relationship with my stepdaughter Katrina open, forgiving, loving, and used the power of Christ to work in my heart to make me a better father for her. God help me see the tremendous value in her, especially since I have lost my first daughter. I praise God for this gift of insight, to see the value in Katrina, although I had to lose Nicole to gain this perspective. As we went through Katrina's rebellious years, I credit my wife obeying and trusting God to use me to help Katrina. I had learned to be available, loving, and rescuing Katrina as my obedience to God the only way a father's love can. When Katrina was in her darkest hour, **Lisa stepped out of the way and God used me to help Katrina see God loves her more than any father ever could.** We have a good relationship now and we are rebuilding our trust. I value her and she values me as something both of us never thought we'd ever have. She is teaching me and I'm teaching her different things about God, His love, and just how far He will go to save us in our storms. I still need her grace and she needs mine as we continue to have a healthy relationship and encourage each other to be our best.

☙ *TURN ON YOUR HEART LIGHT* ☙

In the movie E.T, an alien gets lost on earth and is scared being so far from home. The basic theme is his attempts to make his way back and all of the trials along the way. The famous song **Heart Light** by Neil Diamond from that movie beckons us to –

remember that people get lost in life, everyone has a dream, and we all want a place to call home.

When my stepdaughter ran away from home, she got mixed up with some tough characters. I thought 'maybe she is wanting to come back home, but just can't find her way back.' My heart broke while she was gone, us not knowing where she was, if she was safe, if she had food, warm clothes, if she was off the streets at night. I thought of her as a scared little girl, lost in the real world but desperately wanting to go back to being that cute little girl who rode piggy-back, danced, played, made jokes all the time, and was an amazing artist. **Was she wondering "how did I get lost and so far from home?"** It reminds me the lyrics from the song **Heart light**.

> *"Cause sometimes the world ain't kind, when people get lost like you and me... Turn on your heart light... Let it shine wherever you go"*

I felt I knew she wanted to come home but had let pride get the best of her; the voices in the world lured her away to temptations that could harm her. The song goes on to explain the common theme that we are all looking for - a place to call home and home is the "most excellent place of all." What makes it so excellent? It is the love, forgiveness, and grace a family gives to each other. Then the most important part as you are waiting for your lost lambs to return, the song says:

"And I'll be right here if you should call me."

When Katrina called me to rescue her from an abusive relationship, I answered and came to bring her home.

Home!

The word stirs up many emotions in each of us. For me, it was always a place I felt accepted and loved. I wanted to create that for her. I strive to create those same feelings with my kids, no matter how old. No matter how rocky our relationship may be, my goal is that they each know they can always come home. Even now, when I come home to visit my parents, I feel the safety and warmth of their love. It's the same home I grew up in 45 years ago. It is not the building that is special, just the place I have in their hearts. I have always had that feeling of security. If I failed in my life pursuits, my parents would take me in. We have a joke in the family we were told,

"You can always stay in the garage."

This secure foundation of *home* allowed me to explore the world, grow to my potential, and not be afraid to fail.

Even though I have moved many times as a grown up, our kids always know they can come back home, (Although we would have some rules.) Because my parents had their heart-light on for me, I faced life more bravely and I want to give that to my children as well. **When we recognize His grace applied to our life, we can start the healing and bridge the gaps in our relationships.**

NO PAIN, NO REASON

In Kary Oberbrunner's book **The Deeper Path** he discusses the correlation of Christ and His Crown.

"No cross, No crown."

We all have a cross that God plans for us to endure. It is part of Gods plan to share in the glories of the crown of Christ. He explains how God uses our pain to help us find our passion. Kary discusses how we can go deep into our pain to find our passion.

If you do not go deeper to find the value in your pain, you risk getting bitter, blaming others and living a life of defeat.

We do not have to do that. We all have our own cross in life and when we find out the reason for our cross, we can experience the crown of our passion and a deeper understanding of our faith. Before you earn your crown through your cross, God provides your lesson plan.

Your cross is your curriculum.

Let the pain of your cross teach you something that is specific to your situation in light of Gods word.

When you allow God's Word to teach you in the classroom of your cross you transform your storm into blessings.

Then God starts to work on your behalf. Then you can discover the reason and in the end you will receive your crown.

Your cross is your curriculum that leads to your crown.

The reason for pain is often a mystery. Many people have lost their faith in God or a supreme being because of some pain in life. Sometimes we are allowed to see a glimpse of the reason why a bad thing happened to us, but many times it remains a mystery. Jesus asked for his cup to be removed from him as He prayed in the garden of Gethsemane. In Luke 22:42-44:

> "Father, if You are willing, take this cup from Me; yet not My will, but Yours be done." An angel from heaven appeared to him and strengthened him. And being in anguish, He prayed more earnestly, and His sweat was like drops of blood falling to the ground."

Jesus knew He had to go through the pain of the cross to fulfill the Father's will. His sacrifice led to God saving the world through the power of grace.

- What acts of grace does God want you to sacrifice that is your cross?
- What has your cross taught you?

Because of Jesus' cross, He is worthy to receive the crown. Why would we not think God has the same plan and pattern for His followers? We all have our own cross that is our storm, and in the pain He promises to give you a reason. The reason is your curriculum. Study it, learn it, and memorize it.

When test time comes, you will be ready for your crown. Here are just a couple verses on why God allows suffering to teach us to be more like Christ:

> "Now I am glad I sent it, not because it hurt you, but because the pain caused you to repent and change your ways. It was the kind of sorrow God wants His people to have, so you were not harmed by us in any way." 2 Corinthians 7:9 (NLT)

Then the prophet Isaiah says this about Christ's pain:

> "He is despised and rejected of men; a man of sorrows, and acquainted with grief: and we hid as it were our faces from Him; He was despised, and we esteemed Him not. Surely He hath borne our grief's, and carried our sorrows: yet we did esteem Him stricken, smitten of God, and afflicted. But He was wounded for

our transgressions, He was bruised for our iniquities: the chastisement of our peace was upon Him; and with His stripes we are healed." Isaiah 53:3-5 (KJV)

Pain allows us to have godly sorrow that leads to repentance. We also see that Christ's sufferings cause us to be healed.

When we go through our storms, we can find meaning in our pain and our reason to move into God's blessings.

One day we will have no more pain and no more storms. We should all hold tightly to our faith that rests in that hope:

"And God shall wipe away all tears from their eyes; and there shall be no more death, neither sorrow, nor crying, neither shall there be any more pain: for the former things are passed away. And He that sat upon the throne said, Behold, I make all things new. And He said unto me, Write: for these words are true and faithful." Revelation 22:4-5

THE CHOICE IS YOURS

In **The Reason**, William Sirls tells the story of a girl who is struggling with the pain of her father's drinking and suicide. She struggles with forgiving him, but also with forgiving herself. In a pivotal moment in her life, she has a decision - to forgive her dad and let go of her bitterness or continue down her broken road. **A friend lets her know what she really is struggling with is her own forgiveness.** The girl says:

"I can't be forgiven! Not for what I've done! And neither should my father!"

The friend encourages her,

> *"I know you can forgive him." he said, "and you can be forgiven too."*

The story goes on to explain – she can be forgiven *because* of the cross. The cross was unfair. And still Jesus, the Son of God, died a cruel death to take her place the story explains.

This unfairness works to our advantage and was done in order that we could all be forgiven. Her shame and pain seemed unfair, but so was the cross. That is how it all makes sense, in the senseless sacrifice of God's son.

> ***Do you have senseless pain in your life?***

For me, it was the disease and death of my daughter, and my divorce.

> ***That is exactly why Jesus died.***

So I would not blame anyone, but be able to forgive and live a life without the shame, guilt, and pain of the unfairness. I remember after the diagnosis and even after her death, seeing little girls near her age running around, giggling, laughing, and playing. A flood of emotions overcame me. I prayed:

> *"God, why can't I have that!*
> *"Why is she so sick, why can't she walk and talk - like a normal little girl?"*
> *"Why is my little girl in a hole in the ground? It's not fair!"*

The answer came back every time:

"The Cross"

My storms all make sense through the cross-shaped portal. They are the reason for the cross, so He could save me! I just have to choose to believe it for my life.

While my pain is still very real from my loss, my hope remains in that my daughter is in heaven. All I have to do is believe. She is healed in heaven, and I am forgiven, but I have to accept His sacrifice.

If we let our cross teach us, we learn to identify with Christ's sufferings. In this way we learn to bury our pride as Christ did. We learn we are all lost sheep that Jesus came to earth to rescue. We are all like the lost child in the mall of life, looking for someone or something to save us.

Jesus wants to find us and restore us to the Father. In spite of His desire to save us, we cannot rescue others if we have not recognized His rescue plan for ourselves. Your pain is His reason.

Everyone's pain is different, but still the same. At times, we all think God cannot forgive our sin, and our shame keeps us from accepting his grace. However, when we understand God's plan, then we understand Christ's sacrifice was meant to be unfair in order to save us.

That was His plan all along, to be unfair to himself: *Trading His righteousness for our sin.*

- **In our pain, we struggle with forgiving others,**
- **In our pride we struggle with forgiving ourselves.**

We have a choice to embrace the cross or hold tightly to our pain and pride.

We can be forgiven and healed in the full understanding and acceptance of the cross.

The choice is yours.

Chapter 9

Bright, Bright, Sunshiny Day

"Praise be to the God and Father of our Lord Jesus Christ, who has blessed us in the heavenly realms with every spiritual blessing in Christ. For he chose us in him before the creation of the world to be holy and blameless in his sight. In love."

(Ephisians 4:1)

"Live, Love, Laugh"

Shante, Delaware OH

ঌ *YOU ARE CLEAR TO LAND* ঌ

I was impatient with God in my daughter's illness. I was tired of praying and waiting on God's deliverance. There were restless moments while I was trying to learn Gods lesson. What was He teaching me? I knew the answer was to trust Him in the process. Many days I felt my trials would never end. My situation reminded me of a story:

An airplane was caught in a storm, trying to make a landing. The pilot said: *"Come in, Tower, it's really bumpy and we are catching a lot of turbulence. We need to come down and land the plane."*

The tower replied,

> *"Don't lower your altitude yet. The storm is too rough at a lower altitude, stay on your projected course."*

The pilot yells over the crackling thunder, *"We're running low on fuel and the passengers are getting worried!"*

The Tower knows if the plane tries to reduce altitude, they will run into a much worse storm. The Tower tries to reassure the pilot,

> *"Hold on, it's not time yet. I'll let you know when it's safe."*

The pilot tries one last plea, *"Tower we're almost out of fuel and the plane is shaking apart. I don't think we're going to make it."*

Just then when it seemed like the plane was going to shake apart and all hope was lost, the tower said,

> *"The storm has passed, prepare to land."*

Many times we are in a storm and just want out of it as quickly as possible. But God is our strong tower. As long as we are in communication with the tower, we can know He's in control, that He knows what's best for us.

God is working behind the scenes. We don't know what's happening and are lost and confused in our storms.

When we feel like God does not hear us or at least we do not hear from Him, that is when He is working the most. One of the reasons God sends the storm is for us to learn to trust Him. He wants to deliver us - often in ways we do not understand. Many times He can only get the credit if it seems like a miracle, when all hope is lost.

When all we see are storm clouds around us, if we listen to God as our strong tower He can guide us through the grey clouds. Only then does the sunshine come breaking through our darkest storms. Times were darkest for me when my wife left me and I was alone in my storm. I was faced with being a single dad with a terminally ill daughter and son to raise with little support.

How was I going to make it?

How could I manage taking care of her and my son, working a full time job, and taking care of Nicole with all of the challenges?

Life held many gray clouds of unknown questions:

- How long with this storm last?
- Will the power go out?
- Will I crash and burn?
- Could it get any worse?

I felt like a plane in a storm shaking apart and I could not hold on any longer. The days as a parent with no spouse to help with my dying child were the longest lonely days. Many days I did not know how I made it through work and all of life's complications.

When I learned God was with me in my hectic single parenting life, I realized God would empower me to endure the storm as long as I needed to.

As I adjusted to my single life, I felt Gods blessings and supernatural power guiding me through the darkness. I had learned to depend upon God's Word and faith in Him for my daily needs. When I was least expecting it God sent death as a blessing. He sustained me as I *Endured the Eye*. Now, just at the right time, God stretched out His hand and said

"Peace be Still."

He calmed my storm. It was like the pilot in the storm, I felt as if God said over the cockpit radio of my life: "Flight Ronald David Re, you are clear to land."

Have you had times when you were tired of waiting for God to deliver you from the storm in which you were stuck?

Maybe you are stuck in a storm right now. God is saying, "Hold onto My promises. It's not time to land yet."

If you try to land, there will be worse conditions. I landed from my storm after my crisis moments only when God intervened. They were the darkest hours and I had no one to deliver me except God. My hope was in Him.

One of my storms ended when my daughter went home to be with Jesus. I still had many dark days of adjusting to experience, but the forecast was calling for sunshine. I had thoughts that she could live another 5 or 10 years, as some cases with her disease have been known to do. However, God knew what I could handle and He knew her pain and suffering as well.

A few years later another storm of my relationships ended, when I gave up my control of looking for my Mrs. Right. When I took a step of faith to get my relationship right with God and took action to break up a relationship that hindered my spiritual life. As soon as I committed myself in faith, no matter the outcome, God was able to act on my behalf. He surprised me and sent not only the woman of my dreams, but a wonderful little girl I could raise as my daughter. A bonus blessing! In all of my storms I have seen this pattern:

Faith's L.I.F.E.S cycle:

L) Lost in my faith,

I) In a Storm,

F) Found when I took steps of action and wrestling with God in prayer,

E) Eternal Perspective found in God's Word and finally

S) Save the memory for the next Storm.

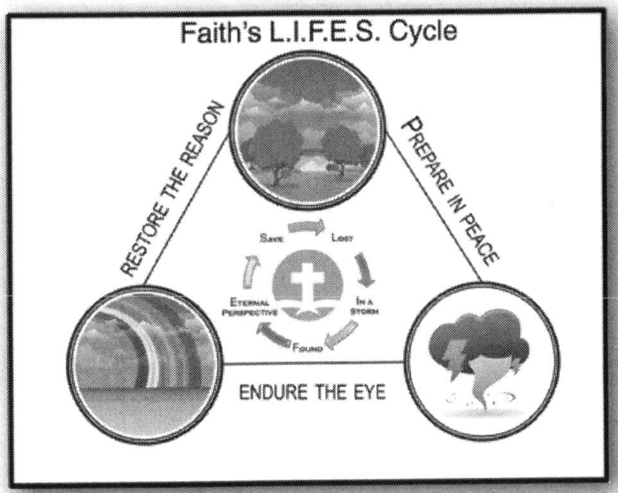

As I went through each phase internally, God helped me to see the reason for my storms and transform them into blessings. In each condition of my life: ***Peace***, ***Storm***, or ***Restoration*** – Gods Word and the principles in this book have guided me through. He gave me a better understanding and reason to move forward into blessings and a deeper reason for my future. God wants you to see the reason for your storms and come through to His Blessings.

- What storms have you gone through?
- Do you remember the darkest of your storms?

Only when it is seeming impossible does the *Son* break through and God delivers you. It reminds me of the song, I Can See Clearly Now the Rain is Gone by Jimmy Cliff.

'I can see all obstacles in my way. Gone are the dark clouds that had me blind... All of the bad feelings have disappeared. Here is that rainbow I've been praying for."

Sometimes God blesses us by coming through just in time so that we have no doubt it was Him working in our lives to deliver us.

It is a great feeling to have trusted in God, passed the test, and then given a glimpse of the reason why God allowed the storm. God wants to do the same for you.

ঌ *GOD-SIGHT IS ALWAYS 20/20* ঌ

Many times after we learn a better way to do something, or have more information, we say, "Hind Sight is always 20/20." It is not possible to know all that can be known about the consequences from our actions. Also we can not always see the opportunities that might come out of a storm in our life. Many times if I am late coming home from work and I see an accident, I think, "If I'd left on time that could have been me." While I agree that is faulty thinking, it is also very natural to question our actions and look for blame and excuses why bad things happen or do not happen. We naturally want to assess blame or give credit to someone or God for good and bad things.

This mental exercise can be exhausting if you do not have a way to cope with the "What-ifs" of life. Although our sight is faulty even with all the relevant information, we can be confident God has perfect sight.

One of my pastors, Dustin Godshall, calls this "***God Sight***." Yes, I think it's ironic that the pastor's name is positively referencing God shall......... To me that is a way of saying "anything is possible with God." Dustin explains God's view of our life as God-Sight, meaning He already knows all of our storms. He also sees our lives from beginning to end with all of the choices we make. God, as the Supreme Being, has a good view of what is going on in the world at large and in our personal world. He knows what my life is like from start to finish. David wrote in Psalm 139:13:

> "For you formed my inward parts; you knitted me together in my mother's womb." (ESV)

He knows everything about you starting from the day you were born. He also knows the stormy times of life you are going to go through. He knows where and when you will fail in your faith. But be confident. God is there especially when it is the darkest hour. Philippians 1:6 says:

> "For I am confident of this very thing, that He who began a good work in you will perfect it until the day of Christ Jesus." (NAS)

He will finish the good work He began in you and in me. God chooses each storm to match up uniquely with the choices He knows we will make to bring about His blessings and our unique gifts to the world.

Author and Pastor David Turner in his book **Seeds of Faith** sees our future this way:

> "Every Man Can Count the Number of Seeds in a Fruit but God Alone Can Count the Fruit that comes from a Seed."

Remember that God has a different perspective of my life and His ways are not my ways. From Isaiah 55:8:

> "For My thoughts are not your thoughts, neither are your ways My ways," declares the LORD." (NIV)

He is beyond human understanding. Who wants a God they can fully understand? God has a view from the finish line and He has already read the book of your life from start to finish.

From my limited sight, in the timeline of my life, I see I'm a work in progress until He calls me home.

I have learned I need to have this perspective every day, not just in my storms. I have to understand my place in His kingdom as a soldier and obey His orders even if I do not like what is on my agenda. If you are in a storm, the best way to get from point "A" to point "B" is to follow the course toward the goal. For your spiritual life that should be Christ. In Hebrews 12:2, Paul describes following orders like this:

> "…fixing our eyes on Jesus, the pioneer and perfecter of faith. For the joy set before him He endured the cross, scorning its shame, and sat down at the right hand of the throne of God."

In the Bible KJV the word *pioneer* is translated as the *author* that finishes my faith.

> *Just as I am finishing this book with Christ's power, God is finishing the good work he started in you!*

It is as if He knows what is coming next. As I sit here and write these words, God knows what I will type and what will be edited out!

When I was stuck in my storm, questioning God, these verses are the secrets that guided me out of my stuck perspective.

I had to meditate on these verses every day in my Enduring the Eye phase. The song **Already There** by *Casting Crowns* best describes our life's struggles and the mind of God:

> "…to You my future is a memory…standing at the end of my life waiting on the other side, and You're already there…from where You're standing, Lord, You see a grand design that You imagined when You breathed me into life. And all the chaos comes together in your hands like a masterpiece… of Your picture perfect plan…"

God knew the struggles you would have and the mistakes you would make before they happened.

He also knew the bad things that would happen to us along life's journey. If we believe by faith He has better plans and our storms are not the end, then He can weave our storms into His purposes. It's only then that God can use them for our good.

God chooses us to be blessed, but we have to see our storms the way He sees them, as a path to finding Him.

From my Bible-quizzing days Paul says in 1 Corinthians 1:27:

> "But God chose the foolish things of the world to shame the wise; God chose the weak things of the world to shame the strong."

In our struggle with God, it is crucial to see God as on your side.

Does God have a plan to prosper and protect you?

Yes! He does.......

..... If you choose to believe He will deliver in His way, in His timing, and for His purposes. Then you will see your way to finding God's view of your condition. Then we learn to trust Him in the storm and believe as Jeremiah 29:11 says:

> "For I know the plans I have for you," declares the LORD, "plans to prosper you and not to harm you, plans to give you hope and a future."

I can then learn to trust others and take risks again. I also can be okay with hurting again in light of trusting God. I can also be grateful for what God has for me - the good and the bad in spite of and because of my weaknesses. If I give him my brokenness and my struggles, He says He will make something beautiful of my life. I grew up singing songs of faith that stuck with me all my life and help me remember He is always there in the hard times of life. In the song, **Something Beautiful,** by Bill Gaither I am reminded:

> "...all I had to offer Him was brokenness and strife, but He made something beautiful of my life..."

This is freeing when I have bad times of tragedy. I can give it to Him, claim His promises, and accept His blessings. The understanding is then – there will be challenges, but He will guide me along the way when I struggle in my faith. Even when my feelings tell me:

> *'How can a loving God let all this bad stuff happen to me?'*

I then think about God's struggle to give up His son and I am reminded:

> *He knows what He is doing, and there is a plan.*

I may not like it now in my pain and I cry out, whine, and complain, but I do not give up on God. Just like When my children would cry and fuss over the simplest requests and struggles: My goal was to let them know I loved them despite the difficulties and discipline. The truth was that I loved them and had their good in mind. They had a choice to get with my plan or I would correct them to restore their relationship with me. If I perceive a storm on the horizon and am starting to question God, I have to remind myself:

> *"I do not have complete sight of the plan for my life and those around me."*

From my Bible-quizzing days, I am again reminded of Paul's words in 1 Corinthians 13:12:

> "Now we see a blurred image in a mirror. Then we will see very clearly. Now my knowledge is incomplete. Then I will have

complete knowledge as God has complete knowledge of me." (God's Word Translation)

Understanding my limits and knowing God is in control helps me to endure whatever comes my way. I don't need to have all the answers. I also have learned not to get hung up on asking the right questions, because I can leave it in His hands.

I can have peace that passes understanding because I have prepared in peace. I am also able to endure the eye of the storm and know that God will restore the reason if I trust Him.

ঌ *SOMETHING TO TALK ABOUT* ঌ

Many times I wondered why God allowed bad things to happen in my life. Like many people going through storms, I looked to the book of Job and found an example where God allowed bad stuff to happen to him. Here is just an excerpt of their conversation from Job 1:6-12:

> *"One day the angels came to present themselves before the Lord, and Satan also came with them. The Lord said to Satan, "Where have you come from?"*

Satan answered the Lord, "From roaming throughout the earth, going back and forth on it."

> *Then the Lord said to Satan, "Have you considered my servant Job? There is no one on earth like him; he is blameless and upright, a man who fears God and shuns evil."*

"Does Job fear God for nothing?" Satan replied. "Have you not put a hedge around him and his household and everything he has? You have blessed the work of his hands, so that his flocks and herds are spread throughout the land. But now stretch out your hand and strike everything he has, and he will surely curse you to your face."

> *The Lord said to Satan, "Very well, then, everything he has is in your power, but on the man himself do not lay a finger."*

Then Satan went out from the presence of the Lord." (NIV)
In this story Satan was up to his old tricks to do evil and God allowed it. Now, the obvious question we ask is 'Why?'

We can see as a story unfolds that Job remains faithful in spite of all of the bad things happening. He *Endured the Eye* of his storm...he praised God and kept his faith even when faced with all of this: his wife abandoned him, his friends rebuked him, he got horrible sores all over his body, his children all died, and he lost all his possessions. It's about the worst thing that can happen to anyone. As we discussed earlier in this book, I will not always know or like the answer to 'Why,' so the next question I ask myself is:

> *"Would God have that kind of conversation with Satan about me?"*
> *"Would He have that conversation about you?"*

It reminds me about **Something to Talk About**. It is about a relationship between a man and a woman and questions whether the town suspects anything going on. But, the better question in our storms to ask is:

> *Would Satan and God have anything to talk about regarding you? Would God be so proud of your faith as to brag to Satan about you?*

Job was the most upright man on Earth according to the story. Many different theologians have different opinions on why it happened. Some say it happened to show God's power. Some say it happened so that we would know Satan's limits and how he has to obey God concerning His children. There are many who question whether Job learned the reason for his plight. In the **Job's Summary** by Jay Smith, he summarizes the lessons learned from Job like this:

> "Then He humbles Job by asking a series of questions that could never be answered by anyone other than Almighty God; for example, "Have you understood the expanse of the earth? Tell Me, if you know all this." God then brings him to an understanding that believers don't always know what God is doing in their lives. In the end, Job answers God by saying,
>
> "I have declared that which I did not understand." God then blessed Job with twice as much as he had before his trials began."

I cried out to God as Job did in verse 42:3

"I have declared that which I did not understand"

No matter how righteous you are, Christian or not, no one, not even Job, has the right to question God about what He is doing, (although we do). **In the end Job learned not to mumble and complained about understanding God, it was not his job (pun intended).**

It is however our job, to ***just believe*** even though we do not understand.

We will not know the 'Why?' until God's grace reveals it to us through life circumstances. To keep asking 'Why?' is the opposite of having faith and leads us to fear and doubt.

Job came out of his storms and entered into *Restoring the Reason.* This is when the storm and God's grace revealed his sin of pride. When he repented, God restored his relationship with God and Job understood the reason for his storms. My reasons were restored similarly in the storm of my relationships. In my struggles looking for a new life partner I knew I was doing the right thing by breaking up with my girlfriend and swearing off women forever. Sure enough, as soon as I did that, God change the plan. I was more confident of what I had done than anything I'd ever done before. I committed myself to God and I was already to be single for the rest of my life if He so willed it. I felt very satisfied and sure of my direction. So what does God do? He sends my now wife and stepdaughter to church to sit right next to me in the same aisle the very next week. I must admit I was a little miffed at God. Then I remembered the story of Job and what I had learned while *enduring the eye*:

I remind myself often of Gods wisdom to not lean on my own understanding and that God is sovereign. He chooses to do things in my life that I do not understand, both good and bad, and it is ok!

This time it was something good. I had to accept the blessing - that I was worthy to be loved again because of His grace.

ꟹ *WHAT GOES AROUND COMES AROUND* ꟹ

There are many things in life I've learned through my storms and God's blessings both during and after the storm. One of those happened while I was in my storm when I had occasion to have a number of long lunch conversations with my boss. At that time Bob was going through some difficult times in his life and wondered how I could have such joy, contentment, and peace while I had a terminally ill handicapped child. I explained my faith to him, how God gave me the courage and wisdom to endure my storm. Some years later after I had moved on to another position in

Detroit while Bob had transferred to Boston, we met up at a company event. Excitedly he came over to greet me at a social hour in the hotel saying

> *"you'll never guess what happened to me! I found my faith and I owe it all to you."*

My reply was:

> *'Wow that's amazing, you found your faith and I lost mine'.*

I'm not sure why I said it, but I felt I had slipped away from God when I was looking for contentment in the new Ms. Right.

So he went on to tell me how he was *blinded on the road to Boston after a demotion from Detroit.* While listening to a preacher on the radio at 2 a.m., he remembered what I had said during our long lunches.

He had been going through some struggles in his relocation.

> *The preacher on the radio said he had a God-shaped vacuum in his heart where God belonged.*

It was very similar to what I had told him over our lunches. That night when he was at his lowest it all made sense to him. He pulled his car over to the side of the road prayed the prayer of salvation.

Fast-forward to our meeting at the hotel and Bob was there to reconnect and encourage my faith. Just when I was at my lowest point Bob was a spark to get me back on the right track where I needed to be with God.

Seeing Bob helped me understand that part of the reason for my storm was to be a witness and that my bad things happened for God's glory and my good.

Bob's transformation was so shocking to me and so unexpected. I learned a valuable lesson from that experience:

Everyone has a path to God as well as growing to see Him in their circumstances.

I had no idea God would use me at the time when I was going through my storm.

In the end, I realized God used me to plant seeds of faith that took root in Bob's heart. As a double blessing, Bob's faith planted seeds in my heart to get me back to where I needed to be with God. In Gods sovereign plan what goes around comes around.

God will use your storm to be an encouragement to others and then later those same people will be an encouragement to you when you need it the most.

ꕥ *FIND YOUR FIREMAN* ꕥ

Realizing we are blessed in our storms can be the very things that end up saving us. Many stories in the Bible depict a bad thing happening, but handled through the lens of God-Sight and leaning on His understanding, the storm ends up for good. A similar modern era story is told by Los Angeles television station KTLA. Here is just a summary of the story:

OC Paramedic Helps Rescue Doctor Who Saved His Life as Baby; Pair Reunited:

> *"Two men who helped save each others lives 30 years apart … on March 29, 2011, Dr. Michael Shannon was driving on Pacific Coast Highway in Dana Point when a semi-truck T-boned his SUV, pinning his vehicle underneath the truck as it caught fire.*
>
> *Firefighters from Paramedic Engine 29 …. responded within minutes to the fiery crash…. Shannon's vehicle was also ablaze and the flames were burning his legs. Fire crews then worked to extinguish the flames and rescue him using the Jaws of Life. The seriously injured Shannon …. spent the next 45 days recovering from internal injuries…. Among those who had helped save Shannon that day was Orange County Fire Authority paramedic Chris Trokey, whose own life had been saved 30 years earlier by the pediatrician.*
>
> *"I didn't know about it until I went to the hospital and started talking about it. Dr. Shannon! And I was like, 'Oh my gosh, Dr. Shannon?'" Trokey recalled on Sunday. "That's when I found out."*
>
> *Trokey was just 3.2 pounds at birth, and doctors had initially given him a 50/50 chance at surviving. But his pediatrician — Dr. Shannon — helped save his life, staying with the infant around the clock until his health improved and he was stable."*

What if Dr. Shannon had not helped save Trokey as a baby? Would someone have been there to save him in the crash 30 years later? Maybe, who knows? What we do know is God used this baby's sad beginnings to bless the doctor many years later. Now that we have a glimpse of the 'Why?', I think about the way I'm living my life.

Am I living my life in a way that God can use my difficulties and storms to bless others and even myself in the future?

Do you have difficulties in life and wonder what sense does it all make in the bigger picture? God can use the very circumstance that you struggle with to end up saving you. You may not be a firefighter or a doctor, but God still has plans for your good in your storms.

When we learn to get over our hurt, our questions, and accept our storm in life, then we begin to draw Gods blessings into our life. In that way we can see a bright sunshiny day for our future. Our attitude can determine the outcome; if we believe God is for us, then we start working our way toward God's best and blessings grow out of our storms.

One of my life's defining moments was when I helped my friend stuck on the electric wire. I later realized the bigger picture of that moment. I analyzed the science behind how my friend was freed from the grip of the electric wire. The experts from the power company said if I had waited another 30 seconds I would have been at my friend's funeral. They also said,

I grounded my friend just by my firm grip on his body.

The combined resistance of my body plus his created a greater resistance against the electricity. The electricity then flowed from the tree to the ground. When I touched him the electricity took a different path to ground instead of through his body. I thought about this principle when I was going **through my storms of disease, death, and divorce.**

In my pain my friends supporting touch grounded me in my storm. They provided resistance from my storm. God's people can guide the pain and fear away from me and lead to healing. I was blessed to have friends that grounded me. That made me think about:

- *Who am I helping to ground that is stuck with a grip in their storm?*
- *Who are you grounding in your life and have a firm grip on their lives?*

If we want someone to be there for us in our storms we have to be there for them in their storms.

I realize we are all busy and life just - *happens*. We need to make the time, clear some time on the calendar, and be prepared to meet the needs of others. In doing so we ground others and create resistance from life's storms.

REASONS REVEALED

My life is not my own but God's and I owe Him to live it out to His glory and for His reasons. Again this is another jewel of wisdom I learned from that Bible-quizzing year, 1 Corinthians 6:20:

> *"You were bought at a price. Therefore, honor God with your bodies."* (NIV)

I came to realize this when

God answered my biggest prayer in the darkest times in my life.

In my childhood I asked him to help me win in Bible quizzing. The sign was a miracle to me, where I had never won anything before. In my adult years I cried out to God to heal my broken heart from the double "D" of death and divorce within 3 months of each other. A couple of years later, He healed my hurt and gave me a new wife who had a daughter the same age as the one I had lost. To give me a further sign of His grace, He gave me a 3rd. daughter with my current wife. Then as a sign of His blessings her birthday is the same day as the day that my first daughter went to heaven, 3/11. I find it more than strange that we all mourn the loss and tragedy of 9/11, but also celebrate the hero's and good that came out of this significant date. This is a sign to all of what came out of that day. A tragic date in my life was 3/11 before the towers fell. Then after the towers fell I realized this date was now a new meaning for good in the birth of my second daughter. God gave me a daughter on the same day that I lost a daughter. I see this as mourning the great thing that was lost, but seeing the good God can make out of a tragedy. When they were alive, we remembered and honored their birthday. However, when they die we have another date we remember, the date they went to heaven. In birth, we remember their life, and in death, we remember their life also, but should also remember where they are going, heaven.

The catalysts to transform our storms into blessings are the signs of faith God sends to us that arise from our crisis of faith so that we never forget.

Whether it is a sign of 9/11 or my sign of 3/11, God wants to make something beautiful and alive out of what was dead!

My sign just so happens to be my 3rd daughter's birthday. So it is impossible for me to forget this tragic but beautiful day.

What is a sign God is showing you?

Have you sought God in your storm for the reasons?

God's ironic humor in these serious events is astounding when every year He reminds me He is in control of my life. We should remember that He is working all things, both good and bad, to my good and His glory.

When you have a storm, try to see the transformation that God is trying to bring about in your life. Believe they will produce blessings in light of eternity. He wants each of us to trust the sun is shining brightly behind the clouds.

If you remember the sun is shining behind the clouds, you can still have a bright, bright, sunshiny day even if all you see are gray skies!

If you shift your view to God's-sight from eternity, He makes it happen even if we do not fully understand 'why?' We can trust God has a plan.

Don't forget to *Save* the memories of what God has done for you and count your blessings every day! This will help you to build your faith for the next round of storms that leads to bigger blessings. Even in the worst of life's storms, like death, the end is not really the ending of your story. In Christ there is no good bye's, only new beginning's. Just as this book is ending:

What will you do with the three secrets to transform your life's storms into blessings?

Conclusion: Chosen to Transform

"Finally, brothers and sisters, whatever is true, whatever is noble, whatever is right, whatever is pure, whatever is lovely, whatever is admirable--if anything is excellent or praiseworthy--think about such things.

(Ephisians 4:1)

ঌ THE FINAL SCENE ঌ

If you have gone through a faith shaking storm in your life, then you have a choice to make.

- Will you let the storm that hit you define you for the rest of your life?
- Or... will you dig deep into your storm to learn what Gods plan is and use it to transform the rest of your life to gain your blessings?

I know it is hard to think of the dreams and plans you had that may not be the same or happen at all anymore, but that is the nature of the human experience. Life is constantly changing and we have the choice to make the best out of what has happened to us or go into a negative direction. Think of your life as an epic drama where only God knows the final scene. If you believe in Christ for your eternal salvation and spiritual life, then God has chosen you to be the star with an amazing ending and a comeback from your low point in your story. God has hindsight, God has the final say in when your story ends and knows you will come out victorious in the end. Your comeback is on the way. Heaven is your eternal home. God will make good out of your storms. These promises and many more are waiting for you. But, that is the key, they are waiting for you. You still have some work to do, God is waiting on you to do your part before the transformation to blessings is seen. In the process of searching for God, He promises to be with you in the process of seeking him.

> "But seek first his kingdom and his righteousness, and all these things will be given to you as well." Mattew 6:33

This verse is meant to help us not to worry about God's part in transforming our storms to blessings. We just need to focus our minds on His word, and obey what is says. By living a life of simple faith, we can then allow God to be in charge of the things we do not understand. He will work about the rest of the parts of the final scene of our lives. The happy ending where we just have to do our part one line at a time.

TWO DOORS DOWN, BUT NOT OUT

My story would be incomplete if I did not mention the impact of my dad and how he allowed God to use Him to plant the seeds of joy. My dad has always had a joyful, life-in-the-now attitude. As a believer in Christ, he has even more reason to be happy in the moment. He has made many investments of time, love, and attention to people in his life that most people would look down on. His impact speaks to a God that reaches out to those that are not the model citizens, the down trodden, and those not living a righteous life. My dad lives in the now and every moment is about engaging the people in his life to be happy and bring joy to each other.

It does not mean he has not had trouble in his life, by now means, but it does remind me of the gift of God of living in the present: fully engaged in the moment. He allowed God to use his natural outgoing gifts to share joy and love to others God leads in his path. My dad reached out to this downcast neighbor to share Gods love.

It may not seem like a big deal, but any gift in Gods hands can be multiplied thousands of times beyond what we can even think of.

> "Now all glory to God, who is able, through his mighty power at work within us, to accomplish infinitely more than we might ask or think."
>
> Ephisians 3:20

I have seen this in the remarkable ripple effect of one person my dad impacted with God's love. This neighbor was just two doors down and involved in some shady activities. My dad did not consider this neighbor unclean and unapproachable, but rather proud to be able to share the love of God in his life. My dad and some other friends from church were able to lead this neighbor to church, and eventually to a saving knowledge of Jesus redemption. While I was a young boy of eight years old, this neighbor had the opportunity to preach at our hometown church. I remember his preaching so vividly as he spoke of my name being in the lamb's book of life. I saw the book with my whole name, not Ronnie, Ron, or just Ronald, but Ronald David Re. The name I was given to at birth and the name where I felt God knew not just my full name, but my full life. While my neighbor preached and then lead me to the alter with my dad, I prayed to accept Jesus as my savior.

I saw the life transformation of this man that now shared Gods love to me. I also saw the transformed life of my dad as the rough edges became soft and tender.

It would be enough for me if the goodness of God ended there, but God's plan is always bigger than we can imagine.

This neighbor became a big name pastor, with a couple of big name preaching sons. They have had a life long ministry reaching thousands of souls with the message of Christ and his transforming power. Gods will would have been done regardless if my dad was used to plant the seeds of love or not. It is great to know my dad's small actions were used to be a part of the humble beginnings that most people would have thought this neighbor was down and an outcast to Gods plans. It is amazing what God will use when you obey the God in faith. The exciting part is not knowing how great the impact will be! We may only see God's impact in the moment when we need him. But sometimes we get to see the glimpses of fruit and the glory of God's harvest of the seeds of faith over the long haul and through many circumstances. This can only be possible by the unknowing hand of God. I see the plan of God where different people came together at different times to cause a miracle in the bigger picture and Gods plan. Everyone has a choice to see events unfold and see it as a miracle or a coincidence of fate. If you look hard enough you will find exactly what you are looking for, a miracle that changes your life or a coincidence. The same can be said in your life. Will you choose to look for the signs of Gods will and transformation? If you do, you will be on your way to your blessings.

CRAZY BUT PERFECT PLANS

One last final thought before I go. No matter what you have been through or feel like life has been wrecked by the storms in life, God still has a plan to use all the bad stuff for your good. He is still on your side and wants to be your friend "that sticks closer than a brother." What ever season of life you find yourself in: God has made you perfectly ready for His plans for your life. He wants to prepare you, help you to endure, and restore the reason for your storms.

The key to surviving and moving through the storms is seeing the eternal perspective of your pain. If you stay stuck in your pain and looking in the past, you will not be able to move to the transformation God has planned for you. In order to get to His plan, you have to take actions of faith that are specific to you. Faith is the currency of heaven. In the unseen world of our eternal spirits using faith is spending it on when we act out of God's love. Use your life and what gifts you have to invest in His kingdom. Just like the little faith I had to give that lead to the times I stepped out in faith for God and the bible story of the fish and loaves: God will show me everyone that He fed from the little faith I gave one day. It may not be until heaven. That gives me great passion and zeal for giving of my life's to the eternal work of God. It is not just a waste and God is keeping score of the good I do for him. That will go into my crown in heaven. That is the great payoff for living a life of the three secrets of blessings.

The eternal payoff that lasts into eternity! I have learned God wants to do a work through me and I may not know what it is, where it is leading, or how my part will play out in his grand master plan. And that is OK.

I know my part is to follow the spirits leading. Even if it may seem like crazy talk. Noah building the ark, Abraham sacrificing Isaac, and the Israelites marching seven times around the walls of Jericho. These are an example of following he spirit based on the situation God planned for a specific purpose. At any other time in history, if Noah built an ark it would have proved he was a mad man. If Abraham killed his son or attempted to kill him at any other time for another person other than Abraham, it would have been murder and a great sin. If the Israelites marched around any other enemy fortress without God's spirit leading, it could have ended up in a disaster. Because each of these things requires a step of faith in action, God transformed a stormy problem into a blessing.

- What is your storm?
- What is Gods spirit leading you to do in faith?

In the wrong situation it may be just your will and end up very stupidly. Use the secrets in this book as an example and Gods word to guide you word to help you transform your storms to blessings. If you look in the right direction, you will find you are Chosen to be blessed.

❧ ***The End*** ❧

Acknowledgments

The Chosen to be Blessed players:
To Lisa, without her support and belief in me I would not be an Author.

Thanks to my children Zachary, Katrina, and Genevieve for providing encouragement, not to mention plenty of materials! Each of you is an arrow for the Lord!

My parents: John and Dolly Re - thanks for the view of life on your shoulders for the mission God chose me to live.
Mom, thanks for showing me the love of Christ in your many good examples and prayers. You are my angel!
Dad, thanks for being the joy of the Lord and - in all you do and seeing the blessings in every storm. You are my hero!
Also for my siblings: Keith – I've always looked up to you and your zest for life. Mark – faithful friend and fearless, and little sis Sharon – you are chosen to be blessed.

Leading Actors: in my Storm of DDD: Larry and Jeanne Smith, Pastor Ronald Greaf, neighbors - William Sirls, Gina, Pat, and the many caretakers of Nicole.
Hero scene's: Kenneth Kitchens, Lenard Nemoy, Greg Bobruck, Bob Slabinski, Mark Frederick, Jonathon, uncle O.C. Rick Hildebrandt, Joe

Sellapak, Ken and Lafone Vance, Ron Morris, Tim Askew, Pat Shatzline, Rita, Jeff Froling, and Clyde.

Supporting Cast: To my coach and mentor Kary Oberbrunner's, thanks for the constant support and providing the structure - thank you for obeying Gods call. To my review and editors: Carol Kuck, James Wirz, Joe Aulino, Jeana Mitchell, and DJ Young. To my website designer, thanks for being patient as we tried something new: Armand Rosario. Many endorsers: Thanks you all!

Also, the support from the Igniting Souls team: David Branderhorst and others at the Igniting Souls conference, - *I put on my red glasses!*

The Weather Forecasters:

Through my life my amazing spiritual mentors:
Prepare in Peace: Age 7- Pastor Alan Dicer,
Patrick Schatzline Snr. Age 12 -Pastor Milner.
Enduring the Eye: Age 20s - Pastor Ronald Graef,
Restoring the Reason: Age 30s + Pastor Brett Kays, Greg and Cindy Bobruck, Bob and Linda Slabinski, Pastor Gary Underwood, Pastor Dean Fulks, Pastor Paul McCullough

To my current Pastors at Grace Powell Church - Pastor Rick Nuzum, and Pastor Jeff Stimpson, - Thanks for fielding my questions and feeding me divine nutrition.

To my Author Academy founding team members. Thank you for the belief in me and helping to guide my on-fire-soul toward the passion God placed in my heart. *Dreams* can come true.

The Rescue Teams:

Members of National Tay-Sachs & Allied Diseases Association, http://ntsad.org
Make-A-Wish Foundation, http://wish.org
Hospice of Michigan, http://www.hom.org
Members of Hospitality Houses, http://littlemarys.org,
Members of grief support groups, http://griefhaven.org
http://www.compassionatefriends.org/home.aspx,
People who want marriage support groups http://www.retrouvaille.org/
And finally, thanks to all the friends too many to mention that gave encouragement and support.

Notes

❦ CHAPTER ONE NOTES ❦

* Childish Belief Section Because you loved me by Celine Dione's
* Is my life planned or unplannedSection The Harbinger by Jonathan Cahn
* Is my life planned or unplannedSection https://hisstillsmallvoice.wordpress.com/tag/40-years-in-wilderness-should-have-only-taken-11-days/ by NA
* We are all terminally ill Section https://www.facebook.com/pages/Dave-Benton/181879061863767 by Dave Benton
* Anchor to Prepare for Storms Section The Solid Rock by Edward Mote
* Roots of faith hold you down in the storm Section Family of God by William J. Gaither
* Seeds of Faith Grow into Blessings Section Seeds of Faith by David Turner

❦ CHAPTER TWO NOTES ❦

* Bullets and Bibles Section http://www.presbyterianmission.org/ministries/101/history/ by None
* Jesus and George - Medicine and Faith Section http://www.propertyrightsresearch.org/declaration_of_independence.htm by None
* Who should fear deathSection Matthew Henry's Concise Commentary by Mathew Henry

* The Angry and the Hopeless Section Praise you in this Storm by Casting Crowns
* The Angry and the Hopeless Section http://www.ntsad.org by National Tay-Sachs and Allied Disease, (NTSAD)
* Saying Good Bye Section Personal Account by http://awana.org
* Saying Good Bye Section Personal Account by Pastor Ronald Graef

CHAPTER THREE NOTES

* Hearing God in the Code Section Personal Account by Jeff Stimpson
* Saying Daddy Section http://ghr.nlm.nih.gov/condition/gm1-gangliosidosis by NA

CHAPTER FOUR NOTES

* Wrestle In The Closet Section Spurgeon on Prayer and Spiritual Warfare, by Charles Spurgeon
* In a Jam? Ring the Section Praise You in This Storm by Casting Crowns
* Learning to Pray Section http://articles.faithwriters.com/print.php?article=30453 by Deborah Ann
* A Spiritual Walk - Angels on the Way Section http://www.centralohioemmaus.org by Emaus Walk
* A Spiritual Walk - Angels on the Way Section http://www.vdcohio.org by Via de Cristo
* In a Jam? Ring the Door Bell Section The Reason by Wiliam Sirls, www.williamsirls.com

CHAPTER FIVE NOTES

* 4 1/2 foot casketSection I'm Not Alright by Sanctus Real
* Bad Woman Section Bad Woman by Kool and the Gang
* Got BumpersSection The A Team by NBC, (Frank Lupo
* Section by Stephen J. Cannell),
* This One is Just Right Section Goldielocks and the Three Bears. by Robert Southey

ꕤ CHAPTER SIX NOTES ꕤ

* Faith in His Sovereign Command Section Hold On to Me by Lindsay McCaul
* Hope - Out of this World Section Star Trek: Into the Darkness by Paramount Films
* Keep Moving through the Storm Section If You're Going Through Hell by Rodney Atkins
* Love is the gift of Heaven Section Tears in Heaven by Eric Clapton
* Tainted Love and Good Intentions Section Tainted Love by Soft Cell

ꕤ CHAPTER SEVEN NOTES ꕤ

* Acceptance leads to healing Section Life, the Truth, and Being Free by Steve Maraboli,
* Acceptance leads to healing Section The Still Point of a Turning World by Emily Rapp
* Acceptance leads to healing Section Heaven is for Real by Todd Burpo
* Acceptance leads to healing Section Tay-Sachs by http://ghr.nlm.nih.gov/condition/tay-sachs-disease
* Becoming Who I'm Supposed to Be Section https://en.wikiquote.org/wiki/Pierre_Teilhard_de_Chardin by Pierre Teilhard de Chardin
* Becoming Who I'm Supposed to Be Section I'm Not Who I Was by Brandon Heath
* Changed for the Better Section http://www.divorcecare.org by NA

ꕤ CHAPTER EIGHT NOTES ꕤ

* No Pain, No Reason Section The Deeper Path by Kary Oberbrunner
* Rescue the Reason Section http://www.brainyquote.com/quotes/quotes/j/johneldred526128.html#jHGFGgwICHeroDWI.99 by John Eldredge
* Rescue the Reason Section Sermon by Jeff Stimpson
* The Choice is yours Section The Reason by Wiliam Sirls
* Turn on Your Heart Light Section Turn on Your Heart Light by Neil Diamond

* Turn on Your Heart Light Section E.T. by
Melissa Mathison, Universal Pictures

ঌ CHAPTER NINE NOTES ঌ

* Find your Fireman Section OC Paramedic Helps Rescue Doctor
Who Saved His Life as Baby; Pair Reunited: by Dr. Michael Shannon
* God-Sight is Always 20/20 Section Sermon by Dustin Godshall
* God-Sight is Always 20/20 Section Seeds
of Faith by Pastor David Turner
* God-Sight is Always 20/20 Section Already There by Castling Crowns
* God-Sight is Always 20/20 Section Something Beautiful by Bill Gaither
* Something to Talk About Section Something
to Talk About by Bonnie Raitt
* Something to Talk About Section Job's Summary by Jay Smith
* You Are Clear to Land Section Can See Clearly
Now the Rain is Gone by Jimmy Cliff

Meet the Author

Ronald David Re has a passion for gaining insights through winning with teamwork and continuous process improvement. Wherever his career has led him, he ends up teaching, speaking and leading others in best practices and self-improvement. His professional experience spans the Media Research and Financial services industries with major global multinational corporations where Ronald is not afraid to take on the tough challenges. He is proudest when he is helping others thrive and come alive in their role. Currently he uses his positive attitude, creativity and insightfulness to create analytic and automated solutions to improve customer service, and improve efficiencies. He works with business leaders and executives to gain analytic insights that drive innovation and better business results. His corporate success evolved from his passion for achievement in his entrepreneur and community achievements. Ronald holds a MBA degree in Leadership and has used his skills to benefit those around him in any environment.

Outside of Ronald's professional life, he is a former member of the US Army Reserves. As a teenager he was recognized for heroism and received a Bible scholarship award that sparked his interest in Christian service. As a way to grow their ministry out reach while in southeast Michigan, Ronald and His wife Lisa co-founded a family friendly farm business

Farmer Charlie's Maze Adventures (2005-2007), now Kackleberry Farms, (http://kackleberryfarm.com.) Ronald's passion in leadership and speaking extends into many arenas such as: Officer of Presidents Distinguished Club-Toastmasters (SOAR chapter, 2011-2012). He is also a former recipient member of Make a Wish foundation and member of NTSAD. He now has a calling from God to share his story and insights to bless others in his writings.

Ronald believes this break-through book - **Chosen to be Blessed** http://www.chosentobeblessed.com is the beginning of that effort as the founder of *Prophesy Life LLC.* With the vision to speak words of life into our spiritual dry bones causing a vision of God's plan to spring up in our Personal and Professional Lives! God wants to breathe life into our situation and resurrect your spirit. God asked Ezekiel to *"Speak to these bones for me. Tell them, 'Dry bones; listen to the word of the Lord! This is what the Lord God says to you: I will cause breath to come into you, and you will come to life!* (Ezekiel 37).

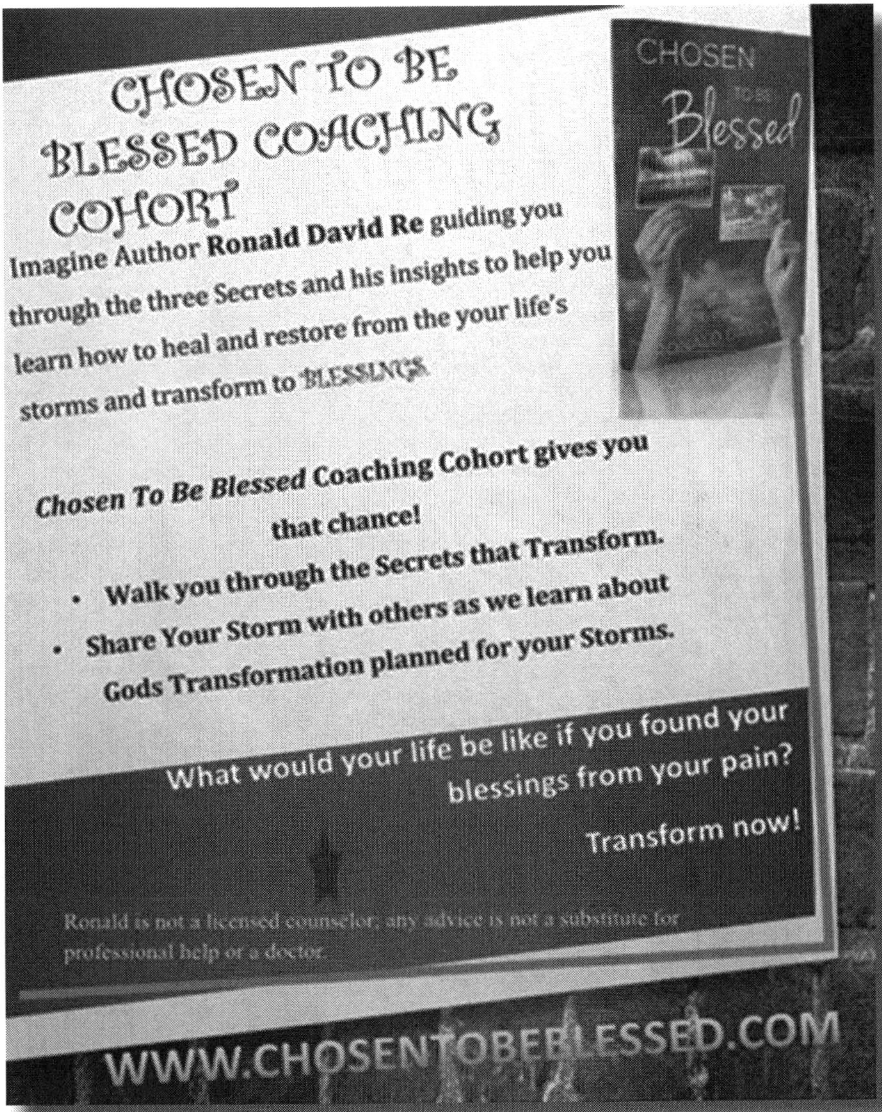

CHOSEN TO BE BLESSED COACHING COHORT

CHOSEN TO BE Blessed

Imagine Author **Ronald David Re** guiding you through the three Secrets and his insights to help you learn how to heal and restore from the your life's storms and transform to BLESSINGS

***Chosen To Be Blessed* Coaching Cohort gives you that chance!**

- **Walk you through the Secrets that Transform.**
- **Share Your Storm with others as we learn about Gods Transformation planned for your Storms.**

What would your life be like if you found your blessings from your pain?

Transform now!

Ronald is not a licensed counselor, any advice is not a substitute for professional help or a doctor.

WWW.CHOSENTOBEBLESSED.COM

BRING RONALD INTO YOUR EVENT

<u>Inspirational Speaking:</u> I WANT TO HELP FIND HOPE AND BLESSINGS FROM LIFE'S STORMS.

I am an experienced speaker. with *Chosen to be Blessed* concepts that bring new insight from Gods word.

<u>Tailored Leadership Talks:</u> I WANT TO HELP YOUR TEAM IMPROVE THROUGH CUSTOM TEAMWORK CONCEPTS.

I can speak to your business or non-profit. My experience and insights can help your team weather any storm and achieve your goals.

Chose **<u>Inspirational Speaking</u>** or **<u>Tailored Leadership Talks</u>**.

Start the dialogue RONALDDAVIDRE.com
Transform now!

Ronald is not a licensed counselor; any advice is not a substitute for professional help or a doctor.

WWW.RONALDDAVIDRE.COM